D071321Ø

THE INDIAN OCEAN
TSUNAMI OF 2004

GREAT HISTORIC DISASTERS

GREAT HISTORIC DISASTERS

THE INDIAN OCEAN
TSUNAMI OF 2004

WILLIAM W. LACE

CHELSEA HOUSE
PUBLISHERS

An imprint of Infobase Publishing

THE INDIAN OCEAN TSUNAMI OF 2004

Chelsea House
An imprint of Infobase Publishing
132 West 31st Street
New York NY 10001

Library of Congress Cataloging-in-Publication Data
Lace, William W.
The Indian Ocean tsunami of 2004 / William W. Lace.
  p.   cm.—(Great historic disasters)
Includes bibliographical references and index.
ISBN 978-0-7910-9642-0 (hardcover)
1. Earthquakes—Indian Ocean—Juvenile literature. 2. Tsunamis—Indian Ocean—Juvenile literature. 3. Indian Ocean Tsunami, 2004—Juvenile literature. I. Title. II. Series.
QE537.2.I37.L33 2008
909'.098240831—dc22   2007036950

Chelsea House books are available at special discounts when purchased in bulk quantities for businesses, associations, institutions, or sales promotions. Please call our Special Sales Department in New York at (212) 967-8800 or (800) 322-8755.

You can find Chelsea House on the World Wide Web
at http://www.chelseahouse.com

Text design by Annie O'Donnell
Cover design by Ben Peterson

Printed in the United States of America

Bang KT 10 9 8 7 6 5 4 3 2 1

This book is printed on acid-free paper.

All links and Web addresses were checked and verified to be correct at the time of publication. Because of the dynamic nature of the Web, some addresses and links may have changed since publication and may no longer be valid.

Contents

Introduction:
Calm Before the Storm

Sunday, December 26, 2004, should have been part of a quiet, happy, holiday weekend for people in the countries surrounding the Indian Ocean. It was a day off for most people, although it was a workday for some. Buddhists were celebrating Pournami, a holy day. Thousands of tourists from Europe had just finished celebrating Christmas. They looked forward to another day in the sun, far away from the colder weather back home.

Christine Lang, vacationing from Vancouver, Canada, planned a morning of shopping on the Thai resort island of Phi Phi. She had admired a wooden Buddha a few days earlier in nearby Phuket but had decided not to buy it. Now, regretting her decision, she set out for the local market determined to find another.

Also in Phuket was Chris Burke, an American studying medicine at a university in Australia. He had one more day of vacation left and was planning to spend it at the beach. He had no way of knowing how much his medical training would soon be needed.

On a beach in Phuket, 10-year-old Tilly Smith was relaxing with her parents and younger sister. The sunny weather was a welcome change from her home in southeast England. It was also good to have a break from school, even from Mr. Kearney's geography class. A lesson learned in that class just two weeks earlier would soon prove very timely.

In the Malaysian coastal town of Penang, Sasha Pagella was visiting a butterfly farm, planning to spend the rest of the day at the beach. Ari Afrizal, a 21-year-old carpenter, was helping to build a beach house in the Aceh province on the western coast of Sumatra, the largest of the islands that make up Indonesia. To the north, in the provincial capital of Banda Aceh, Rizal Shahputra was cleaning a mosque.

The 2004 tsunami that resulted from an ocean earthquake affected countries in Africa and Australia, but southeastern Asian nations such as Thailand were hit hardest. Before the disaster, local beaches were calm and bucolic, as reflected in this photo of a monk praying on Khoa Lak Beach.

More than 3,000 miles to the west, many people in India and Sri Lanka were celebrating Pournami—the full moon day of the holy month of Margasira. It was a day on which it was believed that taking a ritual dip in the ocean and praying to Surya, the sun god, would bring good fortune and wash away sins.

Accordingly, people flocked from inland cities and towns to the shore, many walking but many more crammed into trucks and trains. One train with an estimated 1,600 pilgrims and tourists on board made its way along the narrow seaside tracks from Colombo, capital of Sri Lanka, to the seaside town of Galle. More than 100 worshippers crowded onto a truck headed for Manginapudi Beach on the northeast coast of India.

It was not a day of worship for everyone. Sylvia Lucas, 11, and her brother were playing on the beach at Pasikudha in Sri Lanka. A few miles away in Hikkaduwa, Martin Markwell, like most surfboarders, was waiting for that perfect wave. In the Indian seaside town of Cuddalore, two teams, clad in traditional white trousers and shirts, played a leisurely game of cricket.

Some people had to work. K. Panneerselvam was repairing his fishing nets before setting out in his small boat from the village of Nagapattinam on the southeast coast of India. Some of his friends had already landed their day's catch and pulled their boats onto the shore.

Not everyone was completely unforewarned of what was to come. British tourists Debbie Bateson and her friend Pat Wall had visited a palm reader the previous day. "He took my hand and said, 'Bad news, stay out of the sea, big wave coming,'" Bateson later told the *Sun* newspaper. "At the time I thought it was a joke—now I think it is freaky."

Animals might have sensed something as well. In Sri Lanka, there were reports of elephants bolting from their keepers and running into the hills and reports of zoo animals that refused to come out of their shelters. Dolphins were seen swimming out to deeper water.

All the while, about 100 miles west of Sumatra and 19 miles below the ocean surface, two gigantic shelves of rock continued to grind slowly against one another. They had been doing so for millions of years, advancing an inch or two each year and building up an enormous amount of pressure. Finally, at 7:58 A.M. local time, the pressure became too much, and the seabed was wrenched apart by a massive earthquake.

On the surface, the ocean rose and then fell, generating a wave that spread rapidly in all directions, gaining in speed and power as it went. Before nightfall, hundreds of thousands of lives would be lost and millions of lives changed forever.

1 "A Fairly Large Event"

Earthquakes were nothing new in the Indian Ocean, and most people who felt the initial shock wave were doubtless relieved when it ended. If they did not suspect what had happened and what was to follow, others did—or soon would—but would be unable to warn those in danger.

More than 6,000 miles east of Sumatra, across the international dateline in Honolulu, Hawaii, it was still Christmas afternoon. Barry Hirshorn had just fed his cats and stretched out for a nap at about 3:00 P.M. when two pagers beeped. The geophysicist could tell from his messages that a large earthquake had occurred somewhere in the world. Within a few minutes, he was at his desk at the Pacific Tsunami Warning Center (PTWC).

The PTWC exists to issue alerts if an earthquake is likely to create a huge wave known as a tsunami—from the Japanese words *tsu* ("harbor") and *nami* ("wave"). It was established in 1949 by the U.S. National Weather Service after a tsunami killed 159 people in Hilo, Hawaii.

A colleague, Stuart Weinstein, was already there, examining a reading from a seismograph, an instrument used for detecting and measuring earthquakes. Large shocks coming close together had traced a thick, blue line across the paper. "This is a big earthquake," he thought at the time, he later told the Australian newspaper the *Age*, "maybe a seven."

The number to which Weinstein referred is part of the moment magnitude, or Mw, scale used by scientists to measure the energy released by earthquakes. The Mw scale has largely replaced the earlier Richter scale for the measurement of very large quakes. On the 10-point Richter scale, each step is 10 times more powerful that the last. Thus, a quake measured at

Geophysicists Barry Hirshorn *(foreground)* and Stuart Weinstein convened on Christmas Day 2004, when they both realized a major earthquake had struck somewhere in the world. While the scientists managed to send out a tsunami warning to countries around the Pacific Ocean, local governments did not take action because they had never experienced or seen a tsunami before.

4.0 is 10 times more powerful than one at 3.0. On the Mw scale, however, each step in the scale is 30 times more powerful. This enables scientists to gain more accurate measurements, especially of very large events.

Weinstein and Hirshorn had soon pinpointed the location of the earthquake and estimated its magnitude at 8.0, equal to about a billion tons of the explosive TNT and about the size of the San Francisco earthquake of 1906. They then issued their first bulletin at 3:15 P.M., saying that a major quake had taken place but that there was no tsunami watch or warning.

"FLYING BLIND"

The scientists had no way of knowing that the quake had unleashed a tsunami. The PTWC has an extensive network of floating monitors called tsunameters that measure wave activity in the Pacific Ocean. There are no such devices in the Indian Ocean. "We had no tide gauges. So at this point we had no evidence that there was any wave generated," Weinstein said on an episode of the television program *NOVA*. "We were, unfortunately, flying blind."

Next, Weinstein and Hirshorn used a more time-consuming but effective way of measuring the earthquake. This time they came up with a much more powerful 8.5. They decided to call the warning center's director, Charles McCreery, who arrived quickly, took in the situation, and issued a second bulletin. This one, issued at 4:04 P.M., reported that the quake was more powerful than first thought and might create a tsunami in the epicenter—the spot where the quake took place.

The problem was that the bulletin went mostly to countries around the Pacific Ocean. Although the governments of Indonesia and Thailand received the alert, most in the Indian Ocean did not. And, even in countries where the alert was received, little was done because local governments lacked either the means or the will to pass on the message. It was later suggested that Thailand's Seismic Monitoring and Statistic

Center (SMSC) failed to take action for fear of unduly alarming tourists. SMSC Director Sumalee Prachuab denied it, telling *TIME* magazine, "I never considered issuing a tsunami warning because we never had a tsunami before."

Weinstein, Hirshorn, and McCreery had done all their instruments would allow them to do. They thought that damage from a tsunami generated by an 8.5 quake would probably be limited to Sumatra. Furthermore, they knew that, because of the location of the epicenter, the tsunami would already have hit.

Did the Animals Know?

There were several accounts before the tsunami struck, of animals behaving strangely, as if they knew somehow that a natural disaster was imminent. Canadian tourist Mark Vanderkam wrote on a tsunami survivor Web site about reading newspaper reports of elephants making strange, previously unknown sounds, described by their handlers as human-sounding cries. Elephants also were said to have broken away from their handlers and stampeded for higher ground. Some even supposedly stopped to pick up tourists, putting them on their backs and carrying them to safety. Dolphins were reported suddenly swimming to deeper water. It could well have been that they felt the earthquake long before it was detected by people.

The animals' actions may be why so few perished in comparison to people, especially in areas that had no warning system. Ravi Corea, president of the Sri Lanka Wildlife Conservation Society, visited a beach where 60 people had died.

Curious, the scientists turned to the wire services and the Internet. There, for the first time, they began to see the magnitude of the disaster. Weinstein later said on the television program *NewsHour*, "I think the 'holy cow' moment didn't occur until we started seeing the first, preliminary reports over the wire services that, in fact, a damaging wave had struck Phuket, Thailand, and Sri Lanka."

When word came that Sri Lanka, more than 700 miles from the quake site, had been hit, Hirshorn felt a sense of

The area is normally thronged with wildlife, but the bodies of only two animals—both water buffalo—were found.

Alan Rabinowitz, director for science and exploration at the Wildlife Conservation Society based at New York City's Bronx Zoo, said in a *National Geographic* article online, "Earthquakes bring vibrational changes on land and in water while storms cause electromagnetic changes in the atmosphere. Some animals have acute sense[s] of hearing and smell that allow them to determine something coming towards them long before humans might know that something is there."

Some scientists think that animals might be used as tools to predict earthquakes. The Japanese have done several studies, as has the U.S. Geological Survey (USGS). "Nothing concrete came out of it," said Andy Michael of the USGS in the *National Geographic* article. "What we're faced with is a lot of anecdotes. Animals react to so many things—being hungry, defending their territories, mating, predators—so it's hard to have a controlled study to get that advanced warning signal."

gloom. "More people are going to die," he was reported in the *Age* as having said.

THE "MONSTER"

What Hirshorn and his colleagues did not yet know was that the forces involved were far greater than they had imagined. As Professor Thorne Lay told the University of California at Santa Cruz's *Currents* magazine, "Even among seismologists, we call this a monster earthquake."

This monster beneath the Indian Ocean had been millions of years in the making, the result of a very slow but very steady accumulation of pent-up energy. That energy, when finally released, spawned the tsunami.

The Earth's surface, often referred to as "solid ground," really is not solid at all. Instead, it is made up of gigantic islands that float on a sea of molten rock known as magma. These islands, called tectonic plates, are constantly moving, although the movement is usually so slow that it can only be detected by sensitive instruments.

Tectonic plates are frequently in contact, and their scraping against each other causes thousands of earthquakes each year—more than 30,000 in 2005, according to the National Earthquake Information Center. Fortunately, the vast majority are too small to cause damage. Earthquakes with a magnitude 8.0 or higher occur about once a year and those with a 9.0 or higher on the average of once in 20 years.

More powerful earthquakes are likely to occur when one plate slides beneath another—a phenomenon known as subducting. This process had been going on west of Sumatra for as long as 40 million years, according to a University of Missouri study. The India Plate, part of the Indo-Australian Plate, moves at a rate of about two inches per year, sliding to the east under the Burma Plate, part of the larger Eurasian Plate.

Plate subduction alone will not necessarily result in an earthquake, since one plate may slide smoothly under its neighbor. The problem occurs when the upper plate becomes jammed against the one moving under it, an event known as stick-slip friction.

As a result of stick-slip friction, the Burma Plate was being slowly dragged down by the movement of the Indian Plate. Eventually, the Burma Plate started to bend under the strain, much as a bow bends when a bowstring is pulled. On the morning of December 26, the strain reached its limit, and the Burma Plate separated from the India Plate, snapping upward.

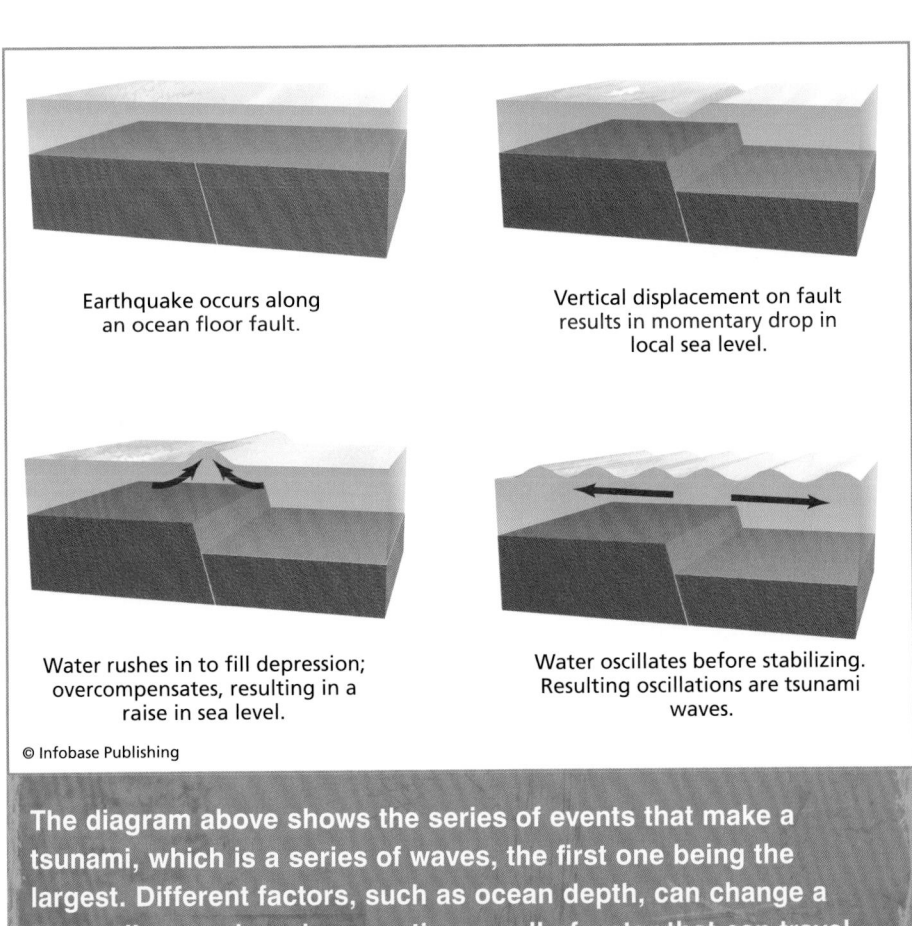

Earthquake occurs along an ocean floor fault.

Vertical displacement on fault results in momentary drop in local sea level.

Water rushes in to fill depression; overcompensates, resulting in a raise in sea level.

Water oscillates before stabilizing. Resulting oscillations are tsunami waves.

© Infobase Publishing

The diagram above shows the series of events that make a tsunami, which is a series of waves, the first one being the largest. Different factors, such as ocean depth, can change a tsunami's speed or size, creating a wall of water that can travel across an ocean in less than a day.

In addition to separating, the plates slipped sideways, causing an immense tear in the ocean floor. The rupture began off the Sumatran coast and spread northwest at an estimated 6,300 miles per hour, opening a gash 250 miles long and 60 miles wide. Then, after a short pause, the split spread north at a slower rate. The overall length of the rupture was 750 miles, the longest ever known to be caused by an earthquake.

The sudden rise of the Burma Plate displaced an estimated seven cubic miles of water. This water, weighing almost 40 million tons, surged above sea level along the quake line, then fell back down, setting in motion a series of waves—a tsunami.

MULTIPLE FACTORS

Three factors combined to make the Indian Ocean tsunami one of the most powerful ever recorded. First and foremost was the power of the earthquake, which was eventually determined to be about a magnitude 9.2, second only in recorded history to the 9.3 quake off the coast of Chile in 1962.

The energy released was 3,000 times that of the first atomic bomb and equal to the total amount of energy consumed by the United States in 11 days. This sudden release of energy caused the entire planet to wobble momentarily on its axis, and the shock waves were so large that they were recorded as far away as Oklahoma.

Second, the waves spread out in all directions along the entire 750-mile length of the rupture instead of from a single point. This greatly increased the tsunami's geographical spread.

Finally, the quake occurred in a relatively shallow portion of the Indian Ocean, 19 miles below the surface. Had it occurred at a greater depth, the force of the displaced water would have dissipated as it rose. Indeed, many large undersea earthquakes do not produce tsunamis because they occur too deep for the expended force to have a violent effect on the surface.

On this occasion, however, geography and geology combined to send a series of waves racing at more than 500 miles

Tsunamis are not born from the center of an earthquake but rather the split left in the ocean floor afterwards. Data indicates the quake that caused the 1946 tsunami at Hilo's Pier 1 in Hawaii actually originated from the Aleutian Islands in Alaska. The arrow in the photograph (above) points to a man about to be swept away at Hilo's Pier 1.

per hour in all directions from the earthquake line. Such waves, at first, may be only a few feet in height—barely enough for someone in a boat on the open sea to notice. It is only as they near land that they become what one survivor, Shenth Ravindra, called a "wall of water" on *NOVA*.

THE WISH TO WARN

By the time the scientists in Hawaii realized what had happened, that wall of water had already smashed into Indonesia and Thailand. They thought, however, that they might still manage to warn someone, but who and how? They phoned the nearby International Tsunami Information Center, but the staff there could furnish no contact information for any Indian Ocean countries. "No contact points, no organization, no warning systems that I know of, in the area," Hirshorn said on *NOVA*.

They then estimated the speed of the tsunami and created a map that would show when it would hit each country. "This gave us an idea of how much time we had in order to warn people," Weinstein said on *NOVA*. "And immediately we started to try to contact nations that were ahead of the wave."

Tsunamis of the Past

The tsunami that devastated parts of several countries on the rim of the Indian Ocean was only one of several monster tsunamis that have been recorded in history or that have left prehistoric geological evidence. In fact, the Indian Ocean tsunami may not have been the largest or most deadly.

One of the oldest tsunamis known occurred in Norway about 6100 B.C. A landmass roughly the size of Iceland—64,000 square miles—shifted under the continental shelf, flooding lands in the North Atlantic. Also in prehistory, a volcanic island near Greece erupted in the Mediterranean Sea, sending waves estimated as high as 100 feet toward the island of Crete and the western Mediterranean shore. This tsunami may have caused the great flood mentioned in several ancient civilizations' texts, including the Hebrew story of Noah.

Two of the largest tsunamis occurred within five years of each other, though not in the same ocean. In 1700, an earthquake in the Cascadia fault line off the northwest coast of North America triggered a tsunami that sent giant waves onto the coast from northern California to British Columbia. The

By this time, however, four hours had passed since the earthquake, and most of the damage had been done. Still, the scientists thought, they might have time to warn the eastern coast of Africa. They called the U.S. State Department, which put them in touch with the embassies in the island nations of Madagascar and Mauritius. Those embassies, in turn, tried to alert countries on mainland Africa.

same tsunami also caused damage in Japan. Then, five years later, a huge earthquake hit Lisbon, Portugal, and the resulting tsunami is thought to have killed almost 100,000 people.

In 1883, one of the most powerful volcanic eruptions ever recorded took place in Indonesia on the island of Krakatau. A large part of the island collapsed into the sea, touching off a tsunami that sent waves as high as 40 feet onto surrounding islands. The waves caused destruction around the Indian and Pacific oceans, reaching as far as the West Coast of the United States and South America.

A rare Atlantic Ocean tsunami occurred in 1929, killing 29 people in Newfoundland, and a much more powerful quake in the Pacific in 1946 killed 165 people in the Aleutian Islands between Alaska and the Soviet Union. Considerable damage was also done to Hawaii, and the incident led to the founding of the Pacific warning system.

Prior to the Indian Ocean tsunami, the two most powerful earthquakes recorded occurred in the 1960s. The first, measured at 9.3 on the Richter scale, occurred off the coast of Chile. An estimated 2,500 people died in Chile and 61 in Hawaii. In 1964, another 9.3 quake in the northern Pacific Ocean sent waves 18 feet high as far away as central California.

Earthquakes and their subsequent tidal waves have been well documented in history. This wood engraving depicts the tsunami that hit the port city of Africa, Chile, in 1868. The wave struck the entire coast of South America.

Their efforts might have done some good. Fewer than 20 deaths occurred in Africa. "I heard reports that some warning filtered out there," said Weinstein on *NOVA*, "and if we were the genesis of those warnings, that would make us happy."

It would be one of the few happy notes in an otherwise bleak experience for the Pacific Tsunami Warning Center team. "When I first saw the footage of the tsunami destruction, I found it depressing and I found it frustrating," Hirshorn said on *NOVA*.

Weinstein said that he almost wished the tsunami had occurred in the Pacific. "The loss of life is certainly something we could have prevented," he said on *NOVA*. "It wouldn't have been anything on that scale."

PTWC Director McCreery was tormented by the thought of what was not done and what might have been done. "In retrospect, it's partly because we just didn't realize the scale of the thing," *Newsweek* magazine reported him as saying a week after the tsunami. "In some ways, I'm going to feel a responsibility my whole life."

The warning center, as well as the entire world, has been unprepared for what took place. PTWC's staff, despite their frustration, had few options. "All of the critical elements needed for a warning system were missing in the Indian Ocean," McCreery said on *NOVA*. And so, as those who realized the danger looked on helplessly, the tsunami raced across the ocean.

2 "A Wall of Water"

Had there been a tsunami warning system in the Indian Ocean, thousands of lives might have been saved. As it was, however, people in advance of the wall of water had no inkling of what was headed their way. In just a few hours, those thousands of lives would be lost and millions of others changed forever.

At first, a tsunami is only a very minor ripple in the vast oceanic expanse—a momentary swell that is only a few feet high. Only the most observant and experienced sailors, their ship rising and falling slightly, might recognize it for what it is and for what it will become. For it is only when it reaches land that the tsunami becomes one of the most powerful and deadly forces on Earth.

While the tsunami wave may not be tall at the outset, it speeds across the ocean's surface at hundreds of miles per hour and contains an immense volume of water. As it nears a shoreline, contact with the ocean floor begins to slow down the wave at its front side. The back of the wave, however, continues to surge forward, pushing the water ever higher in a process known as amplification.

Thus the tsunami, when it strikes, may have lost some of its speed but will have built up into a wave 20 to 30 feet high. This wave does not normally break or curl, like those valued by surfers, but instead smashes ashore in an all-too-solid wall. One expert estimated the amount of water hitting land to be 100,000 tons for about every five feet of shoreline.

Water is not the only problem. As the tsunami sweeps in, it picks up almost everything in its path. "And that debris," said University College London Professor Bill McGuire on *NOVA*, "cars, people being thrown at you at 40 miles an hour—that's going to hurt, that's going to kill you."

SNEAK ATTACKS

Tsunamis can also kill people in more devious ways. Many tsunamis, the Indian Ocean disaster among them, are made up of multiple waves, sometimes many miles apart. People who survive the first onslaught and think the worst is over may face a second or third, often stronger than the first.

Also, the initial wave can lure unsuspecting people on shore to do the worst possible thing—walk out to meet it. Amplification not only builds the wave from behind, but it also sucks water in from its leading edge. This phenomenon, which also occurs when the leading edge of the tsunami is a trough rather than a wave, has the appearance of a tide going out and can expose hundreds of yards of beach. "One of the big problems about trying to prevent deaths . . . is trying to stop people rushing down to the beach when the sea goes out," McGuire said on *NOVA*. "And that happened here. People went down; they saw fish flapping about on the beach . . . went down to pick them up."

A third way in which a tsunami can deceive its victims is that the enormous surge of water, having swept inshore as far as possible, must sweep out again with a force almost as great. People able to hang on to something until the initial flood goes

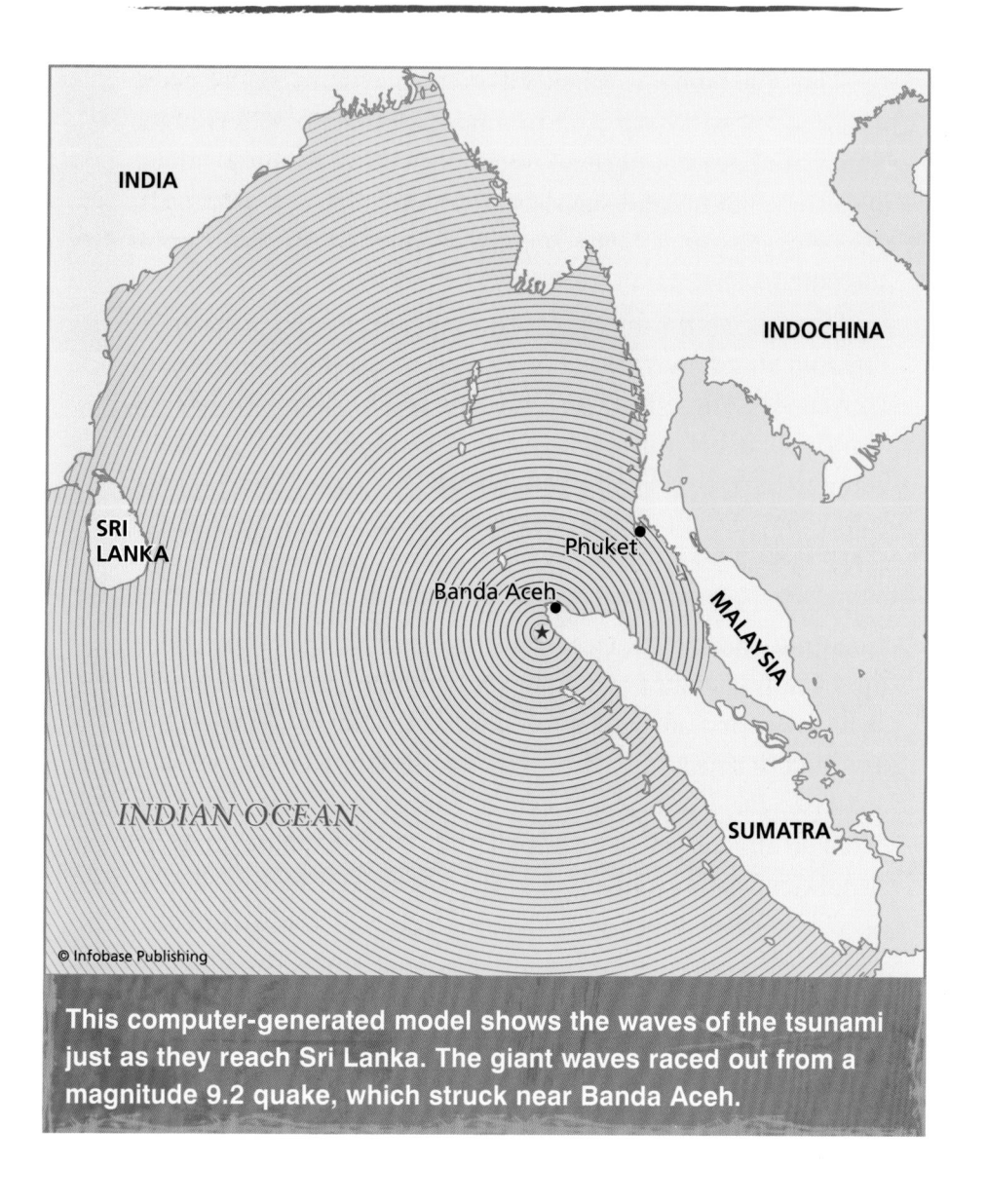

This computer-generated model shows the waves of the tsunami just as they reach Sri Lanka. The giant waves raced out from a magnitude 9.2 quake, which struck near Banda Aceh.

by may release their hold and try to seek shelter elsewhere, only to be swept away as the water rushes back out to sea.

The people around the rim of the Indian Ocean would soon experience both the power and cunning of the tsunami. Those farthest from the site of the earthquake, if warned about the event, might have been saved. For many, however, even the most sophisticated system of seismographs and buoys and the best of communications would not have been enough. There simply was no time. Less than an hour after the earthquake, the tsunami had covered its first hundred miles and claimed its first victims, raging ashore on the Indonesian island of Sumatra.

One of the first to notice anything unusual was vacationer Antonia Paradela, aboard a ferry to Banda Aceh from a nearby island. "I noticed that the ship bounced a little," she told the British Broadcasting Corporation, "but I didn't pay any attention to it." One of her fellow passengers, however, was a local man. He pointed to the Sumatran mainland and said one word—*tsunami*.

THE MAYOR'S STORY

In the city, another person saw that something was wrong. The earthquake had shaken the city, and 76-year-old Muhammad Kadir, a deputy mayor, hurried to a market near the beach to get emergency supplies. When he looked out to sea, the water seemed to be receding on each side but building up in the center and rushing forward.

"The water separated, then it attacked," Kadir said in a *New York Times* article. "I've never even seen anything like it in the movies. I couldn't imagine anything like it." He abandoned his shopping, running from house to house, banging on doors and shouting to people to get out, that the water was getting higher.

Naman Nasaruddin, a teacher, was at home when the tsunami hit. He and his family ran for safety but were overtaken by a wave he estimated as being 30 feet high. Carried along by the water, he tried to hold on to his four-year-old daughter. The wave was too strong, and she was torn from his grasp.

He managed to scramble to the roof of a building and ride out the rising water. Many of those in the building next to his were not as lucky. It was a jail, and prisoners had been trapped in their cells. They screamed for help and stayed afloat as long as possible, but the water eventually rose over their heads.

All along the Sumatran shore, the tsunami swept inland. Wooden houses were knocked off their foundations and reduced to splinters. Stone walls crumbled. The water surged on, sometimes for more than two miles. Entire villages disappeared. The town nearest the earthquake's epicenter, Meulaboh, was about 80 percent destroyed and thousands of its people killed.

A woman who gave only one name, Epayani, managed to climb a tree and then get onto the roof of her house with her husband and three children. Then, one of her children, nine-year-old Wira, slipped off and fell into the water. He managed to climb aboard a floating wooden cupboard and, when that began to sink, got on top of a mattress. "I watched him drift out to sea," Epayani told the British newspaper the *Guardian*. "I was screaming and I heard him calling 'Mama, Mama.'"

Shortly afterward, the house could no longer stand the force of the wave. It collapsed, pitching the rest of the family into the water, where they were dragged out to sea. Epayani was separated from her two remaining children, but they were lucky that an incoming wave returned all three to land, depositing them near a mosque. With water still rising, they climbed a minaret tower where they stayed until it was safe to come down. A few days later, they were reunited with Epayani's husband and, miraculously, with Wira, who had floated on the mattress for two days.

REMARKABLE ESCAPES

There were more remarkable escapes. Water churned so quickly through the mosque Rizal Shahputra was cleaning in Banda Aceh that he had no time to run. Swept out to sea, he managed to clamber onto some tangled tree branches. After more than a week of praying and drinking the milk from floating coconuts, he was picked up by a passing ship.

Ari Afrizal was even more fortunate. The huge incoming wave snatched the carpenter and his coworkers from the beach and carried them 1,500 feet inland. Passing a mango tree, Afrizal grasped a branch and tried to hold on, but the receding water pulled him away and took him far out to sea.

The Burmese Question

One week after the Indian Ocean tsunami, when the number of deaths in many countries was in the tens of thousands, the government of Myanmar, formerly known as Burma, issued a statement saying that only 53 of its citizens had been killed. A month later, the number had been revised upward, but only to 90.

Experts thought the real death toll was much higher. "I think it's very reasonable to assume that there's been quite significant death and destruction caused by the tsunami in Burma, just as it has elsewhere," said Tony Banbury, the World Food Program's regional director in Asia, in a *Washington Post* article.

Myanmar is ruled by a military dictatorship that is highly secretive and unwilling to give details of any internal affairs, particularly if they might reflect poorly on the government. Teams from Doctors Without Borders and the International Red Cross were unable to gain access to the areas hit by the tsunami.

"This earthquake was [750 miles] long," Steven Ward of the University of California at Santa Cruz said in the same article. "The aftershocks broke at least as far. I see no scientific reason why a tsunami wouldn't hit equally strong [as the southern part of Thailand]."

He swam and floated for about an hour—dead bodies washing by every so often—before finding a plank that would carry him. The next day, he exchanged the plank for a small, leaky fishing boat. After five more days, with the boat near sinking and sharks nearby, he managed to swim to a raft with a small hut on it. There was no one on board, but the hut held a gallon bottle of water. Finally, 15 days after the tsunami, he was picked up by a cargo ship.

For much of Sumatra, the worst was over. For Thailand and Malaysia to the north, it was just beginning. The resorts were filled with tourists, many of them enjoying breakfast under palm trees at beachfront cafés or sunning themselves on white sand beaches.

On one such beach at Phuket, Thailand, were Englishman Colin Smith; his wife, Penny; and their two daughters. The older daughter, 10-year-old Tilly, noticed that the shoreline was receding and that some boats on the horizon were bobbing. Only two weeks before, her geography teacher, Andrew Kearny, had taught a lesson on tectonic plates. She turned to her mother and, according to a story in the *Sun*, said, "Mummy, we must get off the beach now. I think there is going to be a tsunami."

Tilly's concern convinced not only her parents but also many other people around them to leave the beach. The Smiths hurried back to their third-floor hotel room, where they stayed until the danger had passed. As it turned out, theirs was the only beach where no one was reported killed or seriously injured.

HANGING ON

Other areas were not as fortunate. In Malaysia, Sasha Pagella had finished her visit to the butterfly farm and decided to go bodysurfing. The waves, she noticed, were stronger than usual. She rode one wave in and then, as she reported on a tsunami survivor Web site, she looked back out to sea and "saw a wall of water coming at me."

Banda Aceh, the closest city to the quake's epicenter, was hit the hardest by the tsunami. Here, a woman mourns the loss of her seven children and 38 relatives in her extended family amidst the debris. More than 100,000 people were killed in Indonesia from the tsunami, and many more remain missing.

When the wave hit, she was pushed ashore and managed to hook one arm around a concrete railing. With her free arm, she grabbed a small boy out of the water and lifted him to safety. She tried to do the same with a young girl, but the girl slipped and was carried out to sea as the wave retreated. At last she was able to go back to the café where she had left her beach bag. The bag was gone—and so was the café.

On the Thai island of Phi Phi, Christine Lang was shopping for her Buddha when she and a friend saw a screaming Thai woman carrying a bucket of water rush out of a store. The woman flung the bucket aside and ran in a direction leading away from the beach. Soon, the two Canadian women saw more people shouting and running the same way.

Clearly, she thought, something was dreadfully wrong. The women joined a crowd of running people, not realizing what they were running from. Lang then paused to look back down a street toward the beach. "A dark monstrous wall of water, two stories high, is barreling right for us," she wrote on the Web site *Travel and Transitions*.

Like many others, Lang headed for the Phi Phi Hotel, the tallest building on the island. The wave hit just as she reached the entrance, and she was shoved inside and pinned against the elevator doors. Briefly submerged, she struggled to the surface and took a breath but then was hit in the face by a piece of debris. She sank once more and almost lost consciousness, but finally regained the surface. She took a deep breath and shouted, "I'm not going to die here." And, indeed, she survived.

More than a thousand miles to the west, Sylvia Lucas also managed to survive. She was playing on a beach when the wave hit Sri Lanka after a journey of more than two-and-a-half hours after the earthquake. The 11-year-old managed to hang on to a log far from shore and watched helplessly as other people in view were rescued. She was finally spotted by a helicopter pilot and pulled from the sea—perhaps none too soon, since she said that a large fish had been circling under her.

On the other side of Sri Lanka, more than a thousand passengers on a train, ironically named the *Queen of the Sea*, were in a holiday mood. Many were pilgrims going to the seaside for a Buddhist Pournami ceremony. When the train stopped abruptly, one of the passengers, Shenth Ravindar, looked out a window and saw several people running. At first he thought it was some sort of game. Then, the wave hit, knocking several train cars, including Ravindar's, off the tracks.

"The water started to spill in, and I felt it come all the way up to my chin," he said on *NOVA*. "I thought, 'Well, I've got to get out of here.'" He and some other adults managed to climb through a door onto the car's roof. From there, they pulled others, including the children, to safety.

That safety, however, was only momentary. While Ravindar and others were savoring their good luck and waiting for helicopters to arrive, the second, stronger wave hit. "All I could see was a wall of water that took up about 80 to 85 percent of the horizon," he said.

The wave smashed into the train, sweeping most of the people from the car roofs. Ravindar was lucky; his car was shoved against a house, and he managed to jump to the house's roof. "My carriage was completely submerged under water, and the water level was rising quite rapidly," he said. "I looked at the other carriage . . . that had been swiveled completely ninety degrees, and I could see, like people still in the train. And they were obviously dead."

An estimated 1,500 people aboard the *Queen of the Sea* perished, making it one of history's worst railroad disasters.

The second wave that engulfed the *Queen of the Sea* might have killed Martin Markwell—if it had not been for the first wave. The British surfer was offshore, surfboard strapped to his ankle, when he saw the first wave coming. Since he could not avoid it, he managed to get onto his board and ride it toward shore, where he was able to reach safety. "I was really surfing on a wave I wasn't supposed to be on," he said in an article in the *Independent*.

FATAL GAME

Another group of sportsmen did not fare as well. At Cuddalore on the coast of India, on a field surrounded by palm trees, a group of men were playing cricket when the tsunami sent water filled with debris such as cars and fishing boats roaring across their field. "We saw the cricket people running forward," a witness told the *Times*, a British newspaper. "The waves were following them and attacked them. The waves went out 15 seconds later and we didn't see any of the cricketers in the water. They were all covered." None of the 24 players survived.

The day was not a holiday for fisherman K. Panneerselvam, who was working on shore near his village in India when he heard a roaring sound. Since the sky was clear, he knew that something was wrong. Then he looked out to sea. "I have been fishing here for 20 years, but I have never seen such huge waves," he told Rediff, an Indian Internet news service. "They hit me before I could turn around and scream out a warning to my children and wife."

When the tsunami hit, Panneerselvam clung to a tree he had been sitting under, even maintaining his grip when the

Meulaboh, a city in Indonesia, was another place that was submerged by the tsunami's water. An overview of the city shows the destructive nature of the wave. Aid workers in the rescue and recovery efforts there found similarities in their surroundings to pictures of Hiroshima after the detonation of the atom bomb.

Charlie's Story

Gary Marshall, his wife, daughter, and two sons were on vacation in Thailand when the tsunami struck. When they were eventually safe in a Bangkok hotel room, Marshall urged his eight-year-old son Charlie to write about his experiences. Marshall then posted Charlie's story—exactly how he wrote it—on a tsunami survivor Web site. It read, in part,

One day Jack and Charlie were watching TV and just that second Jack heard a big noise so Charlie looked out of the window and saw lots and lots of water rushing toward us. Quickly Jack and Charlie ran out of the room and are Dad was there a he told me and jack to go to the top floor. This all hapend on phi phi island and are hotel at the cabanna.

When me and Jack where at the top floor we did'ent know if my mum and my sister wher all right. the hole time i was on the top floor I was naked until some people gave me some shorts and some shoes and i was very thankfull. Then we had a walk to the next building because that was hiyer and thats where mum and gracie were. on the way me and Jack Both herd a noise coming from a bathroom in a smashed up room. are Dad told me a jack to go to next bulding so my dad was risking his life for a Japnese wormon stuck in a toilet my dad sor that the dor was jamend so mm dad kicked the door my dad could not do it by him self so shouted in a loud voce HELP!

(continues)

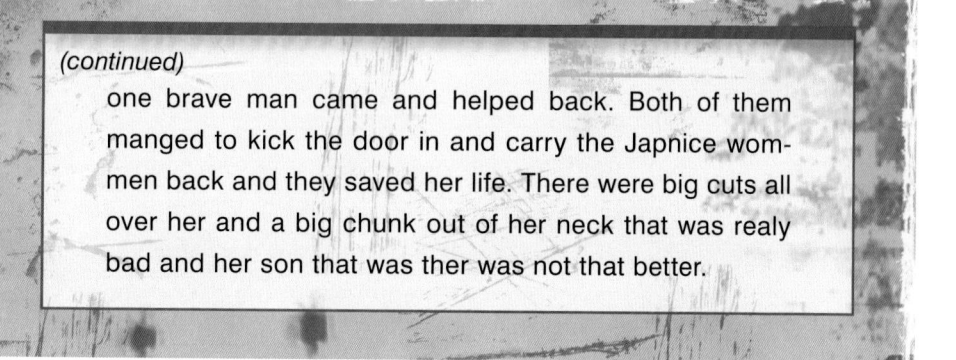

(continued)

one brave man came and helped back. Both of them manged to kick the door in and carry the Japnice wommen back and they saved her life. There were big cuts all over her and a big chunk out of her neck that was realy bad and her son that was ther was not that better.

tree was uprooted. Then, as he watched helplessly, his small house was washed out to sea. In it were his wife, two sons, and a daughter. "I saw the sea eat my wife and children," he said.

All along the Indian coast, the story was much the same. Entire villages were gone, some of them consisting mostly of shacks built on the beach without permission. While the death toll was high in such places, it was even higher in coastal areas where Pournami pilgrims gathered.

At Manginapudi, for instance, about 300 people were wading in the surf, symbolically washing away their sins. Almost everyone was killed when the tsunami hit. A large truck that had been carrying about 100 people was later washed ashore. Fifty of the passengers were dead; the others were missing. One of the survivors, who only gave his name as "Bajee," had tried to reach his young son as the wave came ashore, but it was too late. "The . . . wave hit the coast with a lightning speed and receded only after half the people on the coast were washed away," he said in a *Newsday* article.

MORE DESTRUCTION

The tsunami was now more than three hours old, but more destruction was to come. The waves continued across the Indian Ocean, pounding the Maldives and Seychelles island groups. Dave Lowe, a California native working in the Maldives, reported on a tsunami survivor Web site that "we could see many of the 50 water bungalows that faced the reef disintegrating, instantly turning into matchwood as the waves pounded them, dumping guests, four poster beds, TVs and air conditioners into water so rough it was like a washing machine gone mad."

The tsunami rolled on and, seven hours after the earthquake, reached the eastern coast of Africa. Here, finally, there had been time to alert much of the population. All along the coast, radio and television stations broadcast the warning. Police officers were sent to evacuate the beaches, which were filled with weekend crowds. "I ran out and told people not to panic but to be aware," Mabeya Mogaka, a district commissioner in Malindi said in a *New York Times* article.

Not everyone received—or heeded—the warning. Samuel Njoroge, a 20-year-old mechanic, was swimming for the first time. When the waves came ashore, he was pulled under and drowned—Kenya's only tsunami-related death. "We are in shock," a relative told the *Age* newspaper. "He was so excited to see the ocean and to swim in it. He was so happy. Then he was gone."

At last, at about 3 P.M. local time, the tsunami came ashore in South Africa—11 hours and more than 5,000 miles from its origin off Sumatra. "The sea was really strange," lifeguard Catherine Prentis told the *Cape Times.* "It was receding very fast and then rising way past the high tide mark in about 20 seconds."

The surging water caught several swimmers unprepared. Hamish Weitz was in the surf with friends when, a National Sea Rescue Institute official told the *Cape Times*, "knee-deep water . . . rose suddenly and fast until it was over the top of their heads." Weitz and eight other South Africans drowned, the last people to die immediately from the tsunami.

By this time, night had fallen over Indonesia and Thailand, and the Sun was setting in Sri Lanka and India. Only with dawn the following day would the survivors begin to comprehend the magnitude of what had occurred. They would begin to assess the damage, count the dead, and try—unsuccessfully—to keep many others from dying.

3 Aftermath

When the Sun rose over the Indian Ocean on December 27, 2004, much of what had been a tropical paradise only 24 hours before had become scenes of death, destruction, disease, and despair. Many thousands of lives had been lost; many more thousands ruined. The survivors could scarcely comprehend either what had occurred or the task that lay ahead.

Antonia Paradela, who had finally reached Banda Aceh in Indonesia, walked through the city in disbelief. Fishing boats were piled upon buildings. Automobiles were stacked in heaps of twisted metal. Worst of all were the bodies—floating in the Aceh river, lining the streets, most of them with their arms stretched upward.

As the Sun rose higher and the heat of the day increased, the smell became almost indescribable. "I worked in Iraq after the last [Gulf] war and never saw anything like this," Paradela said in a British Broadcasting Corporation report.

Geoff Mackley, interviewed on *NOVA*, called what he saw of Banda Aceh from the air "like the aftermath of an atomic bomb, maybe worse." The filmmaker, a veteran of more than

60 hurricanes and volcanic eruptions, described a cement plant reduced to rubble, a concrete jetty ripped apart and huge chunks tossed onto the shore, layers of debris carried more than a hundred feet up the side of a hill. "This is chaos on an industrial scale," Mackley said.

South of Banda Aceh, the scene was much the same. The *Guardian* newspaper reported that the town of Leupueng had been completely destroyed. "Nothing vertical and square-edged is left," the article said. "From one end to another, Leupueng and most of its inhabitants have vanished as if they never were."

In many coastal towns, the local mosque was the only building still standing. "You can't really explain," Scott Wickland, an American aircraft carrier crew member, told CBS News. "There used to be towns and cities there. All the people had homes, lives. Now, there is nothing."

While Indonesia was the area hardest hit, the tsunami had left destruction in its wake throughout the region. An estimated 500 fishing boats were destroyed in Thailand along with many piers. The beachfront resort areas suffered the most. Pascal Panuel, a French tourist, told MSNBC, "It was like a scene from the apocalypse. There was litter everywhere—motorcycles, cars, and dead bodies. I saw many dead babies on the beach."

On the Maldives islands, the tide brought in not only dozens of bodies and tree branches but also a scattering of champagne bottles, passports, dishes, and clothing. Two-thirds of the Sri Lankan coastline were affected, with an estimated 50,000 houses destroyed and 24,000 boats (about 70 percent of the fishing fleet) damaged. Numerous fishing villages in India were wiped out and the boats destroyed. An article on the World Socialist Web site quoted a fisherman from Keechankuppam as saying, "The situation is so bad that we will not be able to go fishing for at least two or three months. How are we going to survive during this time?"

DEATH TOLL CLIMBS

The more immediate problem, however, was dealing with those who had not survived at all. Initial reports put the number of people killed at about 30,000, but that figure was revised upward on an almost hourly basis as more bodies were discovered.

In some areas of Indonesia, the dead outnumbered the living. A construction worker told *TIME* magazine that, of the approximately 100 people in his village, only five had survived. The town of Lampase was closed to the public for a week while

Along with losing their homes, many people who relied on the fishing industry for work lost their boats and equipment, creating a shortage of fish in the local markets. International contributions have led to the restoration of many fishing communities, as boats have been repaired and equipment donated to help bolster rebuilding efforts.

workers removed thousands of bodies. But, even after survivors were allowed to return, hundreds of bodies remained, buried in mud or trapped under wrecked buildings. One resident, Marzuki Ramli, told *TIME*, "There is no one in this city that hasn't lost a close relative....If you had talked to me on Sunday, I couldn't have told you my own name. Now, I can look at my house even though my mother is still inside, trapped. When they finally take her out I think I will feel different. But it will never be the same. Nothing will ever be the same."

Survivors, their mouths and noses covered with cloths against the smell, walked past rows of corpses, looking for wives, husbands, parents, children. More often than not, there was no time for identification. There were no facilities for refrigerating the bodies. They were decomposing under the heat of the Sun and had to be buried as soon as possible.

Soldiers quickly ran out of body bags and used black plastic sheeting to wrap corpses before loading them onto trucks, 30 at a time. Outside Banda Aceh, construction equipment gouged out large trenches in the muddy soil. As the trucks arrived, other soldiers stacked the bodies in the trenches, ready to be covered with earth shoved by bulldozers. One such mass grave near the Banda Aceh airport held an estimated 6,000 bodies.

In Thailand, bulldozers pushed through the wreckage of beachfront hotels, uncovering bodies. Elsewhere, elephants were used to clear felled trees and other debris. In the area of Khao Lak beach, more than 700 bodies were found. Some of the bodies were lodged in trees. Many washed up on shore, one of them entwined in tinsel from a Christmas tree. The tsunami had shown no regard for status; bodies of foreign tourists lay alongside those of Thai villagers. One of the victims was Poom Jensen, grandson of the king of Thailand.

GRISLY SEARCHES

As in Indonesia, survivors searched through the bodies, looking for friends and relatives. Billboards were covered with

Despite his best efforts, this Indonesian man perished along with the woman he was trying to rescue. Many victims of the tsunami were swept away when the waters receded to the Indian Ocean, though some managed to survive by floating on debris.

hundreds of snapshots of missing people, placed there by those hoping that someone would recognize them and have some information as to their fates.

Often, the corpses were too disfigured or decomposed for easy recognition. Bejkhajorn Saithong, seeking his wife at Khao Lak, told the *Guardian*, "My son is crying for his mother. I think this is her. I recognise her hand, but I'm not sure."

Meanwhile, in Phuket, Nigel Willgrass of Great Britain also sought his wife. He had last seen her when she left their car to enter a supermarket. He found her among many in a local morgue. "I wanted to take her wedding ring and they wouldn't let me," he said in the *Independent*.

The Tourist Trade

One of the busiest persons in the wake of the tsunami lived nowhere near the affected zone, but in England. Keith Betton, head of corporate affairs for the Association of British Travel Agents had two gigantic problems on his hands—how to get stranded tourists back home and how to deal with those who had booked trips to the Indian Ocean area.

His first priority was the thousands of people on vacation in the region. "There were 10,000 tourists, 6,000 on [arranged] packages and 4,000 traveling independently," he told a reporter in a London *Times* article a week after the tsunami. "We've accounted for all but 100 of the package holidaymakers, we don't know about the independents."

Betton had spent most of the past week working with travel agents across Britain to send airplanes to bring back

There were too few morgues, however, and the thousands of bodies had to be buried without identification. Airplanes came from the capital, Bangkok, loaded with empty coffins. They flew back with survivors.

In the case of foreign tourists, it was days or weeks before relatives could make their way to the tsunami zone. Doctors did all they could to make it possible for some of the bodies to be identified after burial. They took hair and tissue samples to be compared with those from people seeking relatives. They took X-rays to be compared with dental records. But there were too few technicians, too many bodies, and too little time. A British Foreign Office official told the *London Times*, "I'm

tourists who in some cases had lost all their clothing, money, and passports. "We have had six charter flights to the Maldives and two to Sri Lanka, so far," he said.

With most of the tourists accounted for, Betton turned to the matter of those people who had planned to travel to the Indian Ocean. He organized a bank of telephone operators to call those with reservations and, in many cases, offer refunds or alternate destinations.

He acknowledged that tourism in the area would be harmed in the short run, but he was confident in the long term—especially regarding tourists from Britain. "The British stiff upper lip lives on," he said. "Just look at Egypt. It's one of the most popular destinations in the Middle East despite its recent troubles. People don't take long to feel confident about a place again—and those who go back to South-East Asia will be helping the economy; that's what's really needed in the months ahead."

afraid some families will never know for sure what became of their loved one."

One such family was that of Leanne Cox, whose parents, Alan and Jean, arrived in Phuket on January 22. On a tsunami survivor Web site, Jean Cox told her story in the form of letters to her missing daughter. "We went to one of the medical centres to give our DNA samples. Hair, nails, mouth swabs, another form....The woman with her arm round me was crying now....We put our posters on that wall there for Ross [a missing friend] and you. I kissed your picture."

BUSY VOLUNTEER

The task of collecting and trying to identify the dead was far more than local officials could handle, and they put out a call for help. Dennis Hoogenkamp, a scuba-diving instructor from the Netherlands, was one of many volunteers. In a series of e-mails sent to friends and relatives from Phuket and later posted on a survivor Web site, he described how people from different countries, speaking different languages, banded together to provide whatever assistance they could.

Each morning, Hoogenkamp and other volunteers met at Phuket's city hall to get their assignments for the day. This might be searching for bodies, helping medical personnel collect tissue samples, delivering supplies, and answering questions from those seeking to find friends or relatives. Even worse than handling the bodies, he wrote, was collecting their personal effects to be used for identification after burial: "Suddenly it all becomes too real and too close. It is the deepest and saddest feeling that will ever rip through your body when you read the inscriptions inside wedding rings, for example."

The work was difficult and the hours long, but the emotional toll could be greater than the physical. "Things I have been doing are not pretty and I hope none of you will ever get into this situation," Hoogenkamp wrote. "Although it feels really good to be able to do something, I know I will be scarred for life."

Eventually, the number of people killed by the tsunami would be estimated at more than 283,000. Of these, 184,168 were confirmed deaths and the rest missing and presumed dead. Indonesia suffered the greatest amount of fatalities, more than 167,000. More than 35,000 died in Sri Lanka, 18,000 in India, and 8,000 in Thailand. So many people were missing, however, and so many towns and villages completely wiped out that the true number of those killed will probably never be known. As a Sri Lankan army major, searching for bodies in Hambantota told the *London Times*, "All are lost, all are lost. We will never know how many."

REASSURING THE SURVIVORS

But, even as authorities struggled to find, count, and bury the dead, the living had to be attended to as well. Many of the survivors, even those who had escaped injury, could not cope with what had happened. In Thailand, hundreds of people had fled into the hills, putting as much distance between them and the ocean as possible. They spent all day and the following night in the steaming jungle, plagued by mosquitoes, some wearing nothing but a swimsuit. Nevertheless, as hot, tired, thirsty, and bitten as they were, many came down only after being repeatedly assured by loudspeakers from helicopters that it was safe to do so.

Even in the midst of such destruction, some of the foreign tourists failed to understand the situation. Some Spaniards wanted to know, once the immediate danger had passed, if it was safe to return to their hotels. Eduardo Loigorri, who had been helping as a translator, told the BBC, "I had to gently let them know that in most cases their hotels did not exist any more."

Children were especially puzzled . . . even those far away from the tsunami and who had seen its effects only on television. Hazil Moulane and his wife, Fareena, had been frantically calling Sri Lanka from London to check on relatives. When

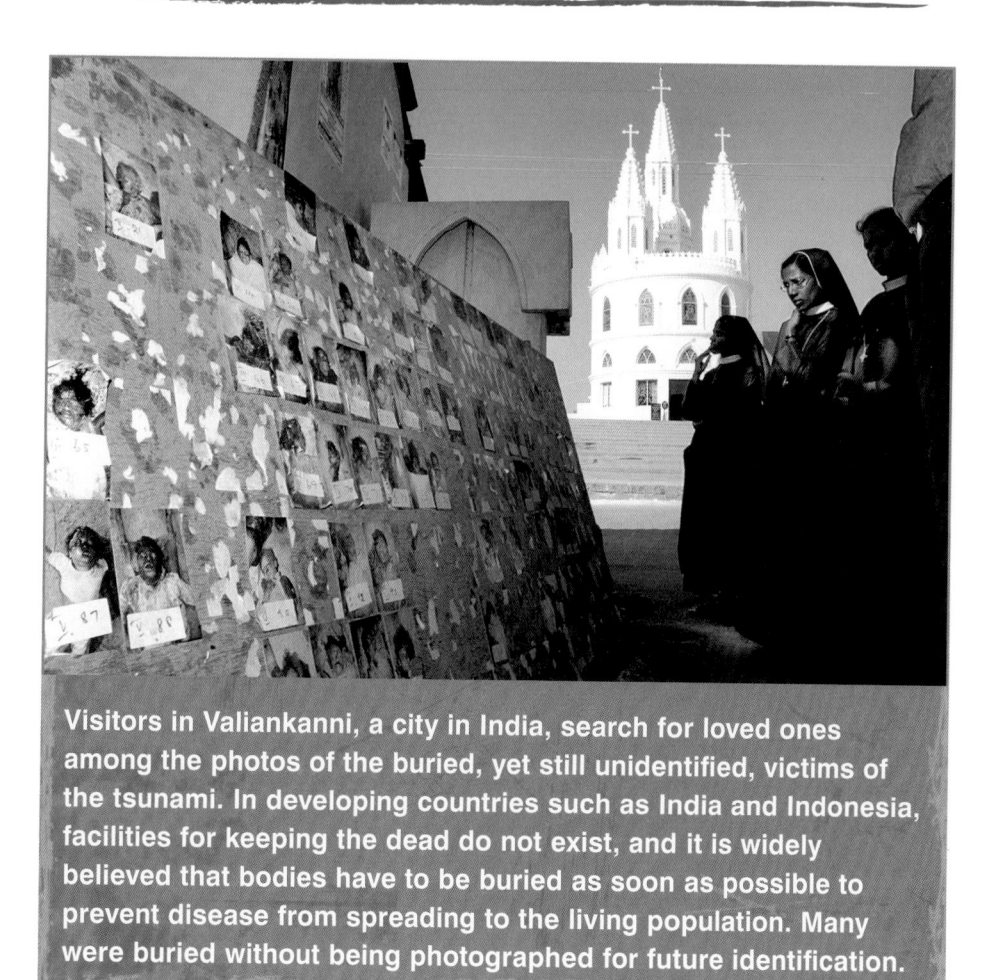

Visitors in Valiankanni, a city in India, search for loved ones among the photos of the buried, yet still unidentified, victims of the tsunami. In developing countries such as India and Indonesia, facilities for keeping the dead do not exist, and it is widely believed that bodies have to be buried as soon as possible to prevent disease from spreading to the living population. Many were buried without being photographed for future identification.

Hazil, interviewed later by the *London Times*, tried to explain the situation to his four-year-old daughter, the child asked, "But why didn't they put on their swimsuits and goggles?"

Eventually, the Moulanes found out that both of Hazil's parents and Fareena's sisters were dead. "All in all," Hazil said, "we've lost 200 relatives. One day I will be strong enough to return to see what's left but my wife says she'll never go back. 'It's a cemetery.'"

The tsunami had torn families apart. Some of the survivors were small children of tourists whose parents were missing and who could not understand what relief workers were trying to say to them. One such boy, a blond about two years old, was found sitting alone in the middle of a road near Phuket. He was taken to a hospital, where people tried in various languages to question him. He finally reacted when someone spoke in Swedish. Days later, his picture, posted on a Web site, was recognized by his uncle, and he and his father were reunited.

BABY 81

For two-month-old Abilash Jeyarajah, it was not only a matter of finding his family but also of finding the right family. For weeks, he had been known only as Baby 81, having been the 81st person admitted to the hospital in Kalmunai, Sri Lanka, after the tsunami.

When word of Baby 81's presence spread, nine couples showed up at the hospital to claim him. All the would-be parents were insistent, but none more so than Murugupillai and Jenita Jeyarajah. When a judge ruled that the child would be released only after his parents were identified through a DNA test, a process taking several weeks, the Jeyarajahs, accompanied by about 50 supporters, rushed into the hospital and tried to take him by force. When guards separated them from the baby, the couple threatened to kill the doctors and Mr. Jeyarajah threatened to commit suicide.

At length, the Jeyarajah's submitted to DNA testing, which proved Baby 81 to be their son. On February 15, eight weeks after the tsunami, they were reunited in a Colombo courtroom. "Look how happy he is! He knows the scent of his parents!" Abilash's father said in a CBS News article. "After returning to us, he still hasn't cried."

Tens of thousands of children were not as fortunate. Their parents, and often all their other family members as well, were dead or missing. Members of what relief workers were soon calling the "Tsunami Generation" filled every available orphanage.

As news accounts of the orphans' plight filled television screens, people throughout the world, particularly those with roots in the area, sought to help by adopting them. But this desire, born out of kindness and pity, would take on darker aspects. A black market, or illegal trade, for children quickly developed. Shadowy figures and bogus agencies promised, for a price, to arrange adoptions.

Some of the people showing up at orphanages to claim children were, indeed, relatives. Others were not. In one Sri Lankan refugee center, officials reported offers to buy children. A couple in Banda Aceh succeeded in getting away with a four-year-old boy after claiming he was their son. "Bad people take advantage of difficult situations," Carol Bellamy of the relief agency UNICEF told *TIME*.

Governments in the tsunami region reacted by allowing adoption only after a very thorough screening process and almost never allowed children to leave their home countries unless it was to join a relative when no other relatives could be found. "We are concerned with the movement of children as commodities, and so we do not support systems that allow orphans to be essentially sold," Martin Dawes of UNICEF told the *Christian Science Monitor*. "And we don't want parents that bypass the legal process, pay top dollar . . . where there is no accountability by the parent or agent."

TREATING THE INJURED

Adult survivors had their problems, too, especially the thousands of injured who needed immediate treatment. Many of those who had escaped drowning had suffered broken bones from having been hurled into trees or buildings. Many others had suffered cuts from pieces of metal swirling in the flood. Doctors, nurses, and hospital facilities were quickly overwhelmed and called for volunteers.

Among those helping treat the wounded was Chris Burke, an Australian medical student. When the tsunami's waves had finally receded, Burke and other volunteers set up a makeshift first-aid center in the Phi Phi Hotel. In an article written for *Pacific*, the magazine of his American university, he said, "People were laid out with crush injuries, huge lacerations with bones exposed, people who had lost large amounts of blood, fractures, head injuries, people in shock and many other injuries."

Burke and the others rounded up what medical supplies they could and treated the worst of the injuries until Thai army helicopters arrived with more help. He then went to the helicopters' landing place to assist with triage—making quick observations of the injured and classifying them as to the urgency of their need for care. It was an international effort, people from different countries, speaking different languages, all trying to cope with what seemed like a never-ending stream of patients. A Swede directed incoming traffic while Burke, a psychiatrist from London, a doctor from Canada, and a Spanish-speaking emergency medical technician provided treatment.

"By looking at someone for five seconds you could see the amount of physical and emotional pain they were experiencing," Burke wrote, "but there's only so much you can do. Just holding their hand can make the biggest difference."

Many survivors had nothing but praise for the effort put forth by the Thai government and for the kindness of the people. Burke, who had suffered a foot injury, was eventually airlifted to the city of Krabi and was extremely impressed with the efficiency of the medical teams there. Even organization, however, sometimes could not overcome the problem of communication between doctors and patients who spoke different languages. Londoner Luke Simmons, writing on a survivor Web site, said, "I love the Thai people. They are simply one of the, if not THE, kindest races out there, but in our hospital language was a problem. In the intensive care unit not one of the nurses spoke English."

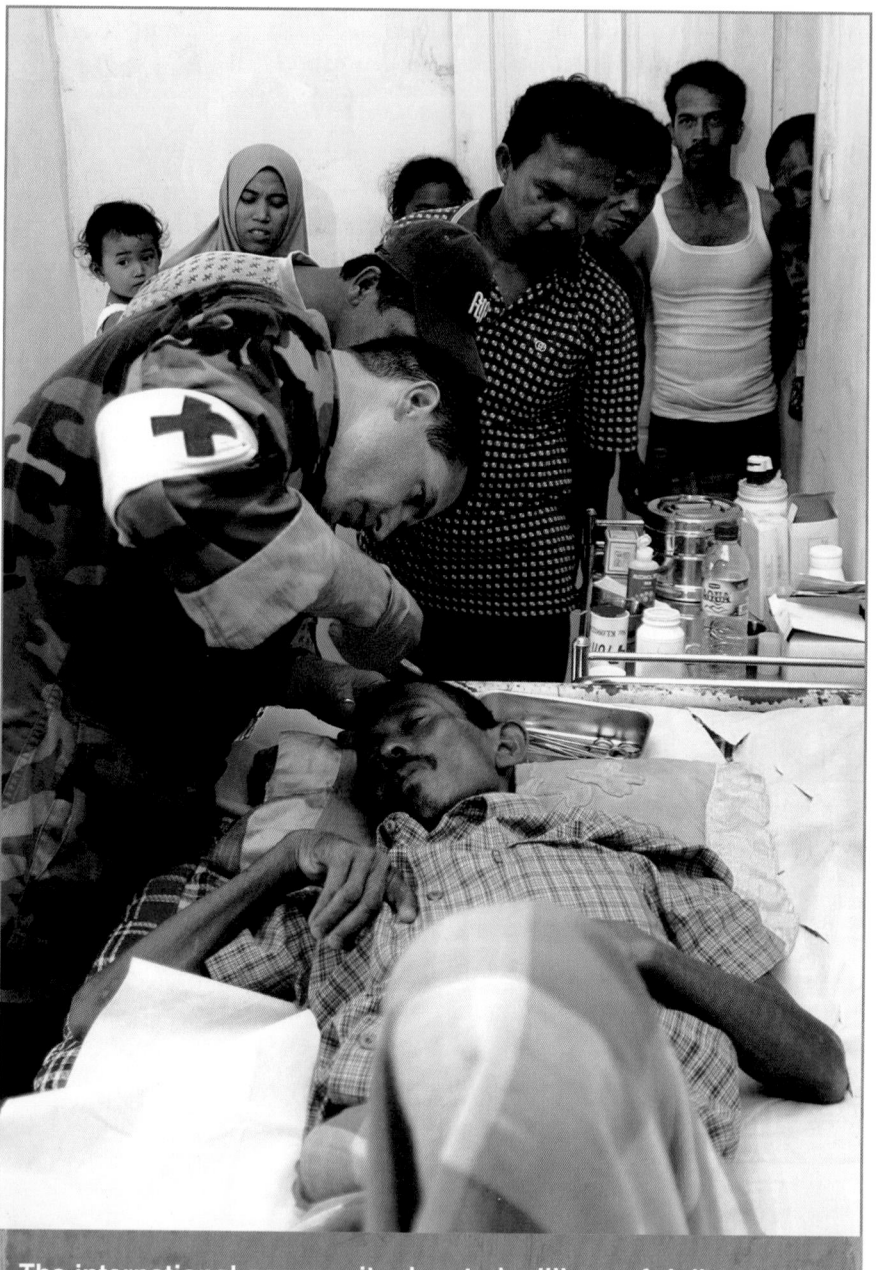

The international community donated millions of dollars to the countries affected by the tsunami and sent out medical teams to the hardest-hit areas. Here, a member of the U.S. Navy treats an Indonesian man.

Another British citizen, who only used his first name, Felix, when posting his story, also was struck by the way the people of Thailand treated their guests. He had been on Phi Phi and finally was able to take a ferry to Phuket. There, he found "pandemonium, lots of noise and sirens and the Thai people thrusting dishes of noodles and rice at us. They were so lovely and genuine and kind to us, strangers, when their own country had been devastated."

THE HOMELESS

Even those who had escaped injury had their share of problems. The tsunami had displaced an estimated 5 million people from Indonesia to Africa. They had no place to live, no belongings, and no means of livelihood. In Akkarapettai, India, fisherman Raja Krishnamurthy sadly surveyed his wrecked fishing craft, which had been uninsured. "This is the first boat I owned in my life. The boat was my pride," he told the *Washington Post*. "Today my boat is nothing by scrap, to be weighed and sold."

Water was scarce in places, the inrushing saltwater having contaminated most sources of supply. Food in freezers and refrigerators lasted only a day at most with electric power out. In Banda Aceh, hungry crowds broke into grocery stores only to find the food ruined by water and mud.

Transportation was almost nonexistent. Roads were impassable in most coastal areas, and even where there were roads, all available gasoline for vehicles was quickly used up. Only two gasoline stations were open in Banda Aceh, and the army placed armed guards at both.

Thailand, despite praise for the kindness of its citizens, was the scene of widespread looting. Intruders took advantage of the chaos to pilfer tourists' belongings and other items from luxury hotels. Looters also ransacked houses and shops in Banda Aceh, stopping only when the army gave soldiers orders to shoot looters on sight.

The Sea Mother

Among the people most affected by the tsunami were the fishermen living in small villages along the northeastern coast of India. When a *Washington Post* reporter visited the town of Akkarapettai, he found a mixture of optimism and resignation.

It had been three weeks since the giant waves wrecked their village and many of the fishing boats on which their lives depended, and the people were wondering what kind of future awaited them. "It is an old habit for us to come to the sea at dawn, except there is no work now," said Manmaga Kalaimani. "The conversation is usually about death, or about the wreckage of our boats."

One fisherman, Sinnapu Seveusettiyar, was optimistic. "We have no other skills but fishing. Only after we get the compensation [from the government] can we buy new boats. The sea mother will be generous to us again."

But Seveusettiyar's wife, Kasiamma, disagreed. "I trusted the sea all my life, but look where she brought us," she said. "Do not say sea mother again."

At that, another fisherman, Raja Krishnamurthy, said, "We are fishermen; how can we stop trusting the sea?"

While some of the looters were criminals out for profit, others were simply trying to find the means to stay alive. Red Cross official Irman Rachmat said in an Associated Press article that people on Sumatra were in despair. "People are looting, but not because they are evil, but they are hungry," he said.

People were also homeless. An estimated 5 million people had their homes destroyed or damaged beyond repair. Until refugee centers could be established, many of them did not know from one night to the next where they would be sleeping. Some moved in with relatives. Others, who no longer had relatives, took shelter wherever they could—mostly in churches, mosques, and schools. Bhagya Lakshmi, an Indian fisherman's wife, was placed first in a Buddhist temple, then a school, and finally a wedding hall. "Now they say we have to move again because they want to conduct marriages here," she said in a World Socialist Web site article. "I don't know how I'll manage this little one [indicating a crying baby] and another son in this way."

The tsunami survivors coped however they could. They buried their dead when they could find them. Their wounds—the physical wounds, at least—began to heal. But, even as they turned to face the future, they paused to remember those who had been lost. On shores in India, hundreds gathered to throw flower petals into the sea and pray that somehow those missing might return. Dennis Hoogenkamp attended a memorial service at the end of which 2,000 lighted candles were attached to balloons and released to sail into the sky. An elderly Thai man nearby told him, "Don't be sad, just let them go to heaven. It's all over now."

4 Disease: "The Second Wave"

O nce the waters receded and badly wounded survivors received emergency care, the people of the Indian Ocean region might have thought the worst was over. Others had different thoughts. "The initial terror associated with the tsunami and the earthquake itself may be dwarfed by the longer-term suffering of the affected communities," Dr. David Nabarro, head of crisis operations for the World Health Organization (WHO), said in a *Sydney (Australia) Morning Herald* article. "There is certainly a chance we could have as many dying from communicable diseases as from the tsunami."

Dr. Nabarro's statement drew widespread media attention and was echoed by other experts. In a *Sydney Morning Herald* article headlined "Second wave of horror in diseases," Professor Joseph McCormack, head of the Australasian Society for Infectious Diseases, said, "If you look back with other comparable disasters, with flooding and loss of sewage services, and the loss of ability to guarantee clean water ... you can't see this being anything other than a major disaster."

On January 2, exactly a week after the tsunami, WHO issued a report in which the organization outlined its major concerns.

Chief among them was those diseases transmitted by contaminated drinking water—cholera, typhoid fever, shigellosis, and hepatitis A and E. Of these, cholera and typhoid fever were considered the most serious. Both cholera and typhoid germs are passed out of the body in feces or urine, and contagion occurs when such waste products contaminate water supplies.

Cholera kills tens of thousands of people each year, most of them in Africa and in the region affected by the tsunami. Victims suffer severe diarrhea, and adults may lose up to two gallons of body fluid a day. In some cases, death from dehydration can occur within hours.

Typhoid is less deadly than cholera, but still can be fatal—especially to children—if not treated quickly with antibiotics. The disease attacks the intestinal tract, causing severe inflammation and high fever.

THE BURIAL QUESTION

Many people assumed, and numerous news media reported, that the chance of cholera and typhoid fever epidemics would be increased because of the number of unburied bodies or the bodies placed in mass graves. "People repeat so often that bodies have to be disposed of to protect public health that people assume it must be true," said Oliver Morgan of the London School of Tropical Medicine and Hygiene in an article on NewScientist.com.

Actually, however, decomposing bodies contribute little or nothing to the spread of such communicable diseases as cholera and typhoid fever. "Someone who died without cholera isn't suddenly going to generate it," said Jean-Luc Poncelet of WHO's Pan-American Health Organization in an article on the NewScientist Web site. He added that even if the deceased person did have cholera or some other infectious disease, the disease germs live only a short time after the person dies.

This was not to say, however, that the threat of cholera, typhoid, and the other waterborne diseases did not exist.

Sewage and water treatment plants had been disabled by the flood. The makeshift camps in which thousands of displaced people gathered often lacked sanitation facilities, forcing residents to use open latrines. The United Nations Children's Fund (UNICEF) estimated that in some areas of Indonesia only one of every thousand people had access to a toilet. "The conditions in Indonesia and the other countries affected were absolutely fertile for people to get diarrhea and other infections," WHO's Nabarro said in a BBC article.

The World Health Organization also warned against outbreaks of malaria and dengue fever. Both diseases are spread by mosquitoes, and it was feared that the tsunami had left

Taken in 2006, this picture shows Thai workers burying the last of the unidentified victims of the tsunami disaster. Many of these victims are believed to be migrant workers from Myanmar, whose families could not afford to travel to Thailand to claim the bodies.

behind a large number of pools and boggy areas where mosquitoes might breed. Both malaria and dengue fever can have high fatality rates among children.

At least one expert disagreed with the predictions of an malaria outbreak. Dr. Stephen Morse of Columbia University told ABC News, "The risk of mosquito-borne diseases is relatively low." He noted that most of the standing water left by the tsunami was from the ocean and that mosquitoes could not breed in saltwater. He warned, however, that "it's something to be very careful about later on."

"TSUNAMI LUNG"

The tsunami produced at least one unforeseen health problem. Many who had survived being inundated by the waves had, as they struggled, breathed in a combination of seawater and dirt. In some cases, this mixture was polluted, and bacteria moved from the lungs through the nervous system to the brain, resulting in paralysis. Doctors termed the condition *tsunami lung*.

Diseases were not the only concern of health officials. Thousands of people injured in the tsunami had only very limited access to first aid, and those with even small wounds ran a high risk of infection, especially because of the lack of sanitation. Interviewed on the Cable News Network (CNN), Dr. Phyllis Kozarsky of the Emory University School of Medicine said, "One of the things that I think people sometimes overlook is just simple injuries, the scratches and abrasions that people have from being tossed about in the water—simple now, but can become aggravated."

Nevertheless, one of the most urgent tasks facing health officials was to provide clean, safe drinking water. While it was possible in some areas to bring in large amounts of water, either in bottles or large containers, some of the hardest-hit places were inaccessible because ports or airports had been destroyed and roads made impassable. In such areas, officials turned to a chemical process known as flocculation.

Flocculation is a two-step process. First, the water is treated with chemical agents (usually compounds of iron, aluminum, calcium, or magnesium) that cause dirt and other impurities in the water to cluster into what are called "flocs."

Lives in the Midst of Death

The medical crisis in many areas affected by the tsunami involved not only those with serious illnesses or injuries but also thousands of people, such as pregnant women, who needed routine medical care. The World Health Organization (WHO) estimated in February 2005 that about 40,000 pregnant women had been left homeless by the tsunami. As a result, when WHO sent teams of health professionals into the stricken areas, it made sure that those teams included obstetricians, doctors, and nurses specializing in newborn babies.

"We need to provide skilled care to these 40,000 mothers-to-be, and pay special attention to the thousands of new lives coming into the world in the coming weeks," Joy Phumaphi, WHO's assistant director for general, family, and community health, said in an Environmental News Service article: "Timely access to health facilities and services for mothers and babies must be a priority."

"Even under normal circumstances, maternal and child health is a matter of major concern in the region," added Dr. Samlee Plianbangchang, WHO's Southeast Asia regional director. "Maternal deaths in this region account for one-third of the total number of . . . deaths and over three million children die below the age of five in this region annually, mostly from preventable causes. The tsunami has further added to the pressure.

This clustering makes it far easier to filter the water. The next step in the process is to add small amounts of chlorine bleach to the filtered water. The bleach kills any remaining bacteria, making the water safe to drink.

The chief problem with flocculation in the tsunami zone was that it was time consuming. It was difficult to treat large volumes, and the amount of water purified seldom met the demand. In addition, the chemicals needed for the process had to be imported in most cases and were expensive. UNICEF did what it could, shipping in supplies of chlorine tablets, but the long-range solution to the water problem was to restore both the sewage and water treatment plants in addition to area wells.

Restoring wells was particularly important to rural areas that lacked the water supply and treatment facilities available to cities. It was, however, a slow process. In Sri Lanka, officials began a program of pumping wells clear of the seawater deposited by the tsunami. In some cases, too much water was pumped out, and seawater from underground aquifers seeped back into the wells. Elsewhere, the seawater was pumped to reservoirs too close to the wells and seeped back into them. Another problem was that many of the wells did not have reinforced walls and collapsed under the strain of the pumping. An international team of experts visiting Sri Lanka three months after the tsunami reported that the salt level in most wells being pumped had declined very little.

Governments made plans to pipe water to rural areas, but it would be many months before such projects could take effect in some areas. In the meantime, private companies did what they could. General Electric Corporation set up a water purification plant in India that produced more than 100,000 gallons a day that the company then transported to hospitals, orphanages, and refugee camps. The Lion Brewery in Sri Lanka did its part, converting its plant to bottle water instead of beer. "With so much loss of life, how could you not help,"

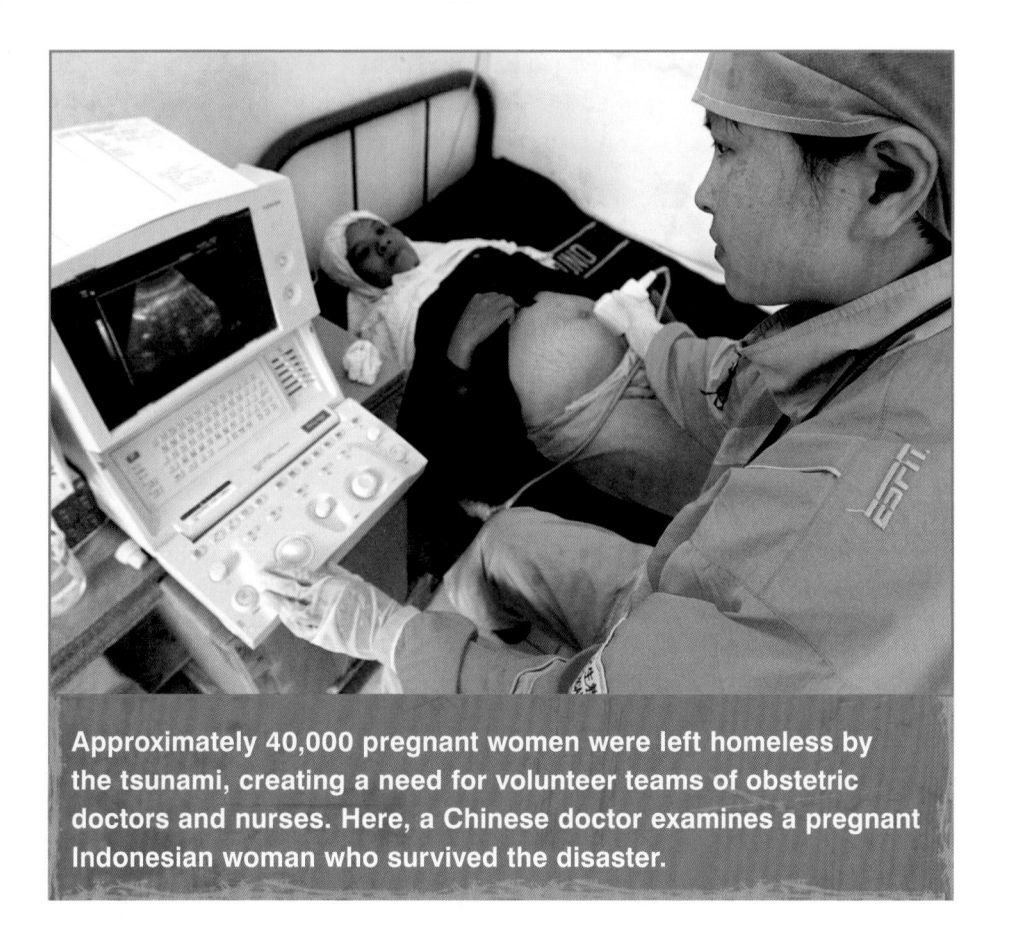

Approximately 40,000 pregnant women were left homeless by the tsunami, creating a need for volunteer teams of obstetric doctors and nurses. Here, a Chinese doctor examines a pregnant Indonesian woman who survived the disaster.

the brewery's manager, Nausha Raheem, said in an article in *Pub Speak*, a British newsletter. "Once we got over the initial shock and realized the gravity of the situation, we decided to do what we could to help."

THE NEED FOR DRUGS

Water was not the only thing in short supply. In the first few days after the tsunami, hospitals' supply of drugs and vaccine was depleted. The World Health Organization, particularly worried about a possible cholera epidemic, sought help from Sweden, the only country in the world with stockpiles of cholera vaccine. The Swedish government responded by shipping enough vaccine to Sri Lanka and southern India to provide inoculations for 200,000 people.

Several drug companies moved quickly to make contributions. Pfizer, Inc., gave $3 million in cash and $25 million worth of medicines. Merck & Company gave $3 million and said it would also donate drugs. Closer to the scene of destruction, the Indonesian drug company Bio Farma sent 15,000 doses of typhoid vaccine into Aceh province.

Drug companies were not the only ones helping to increase supplies. Members of a pharmacists' organization in Great

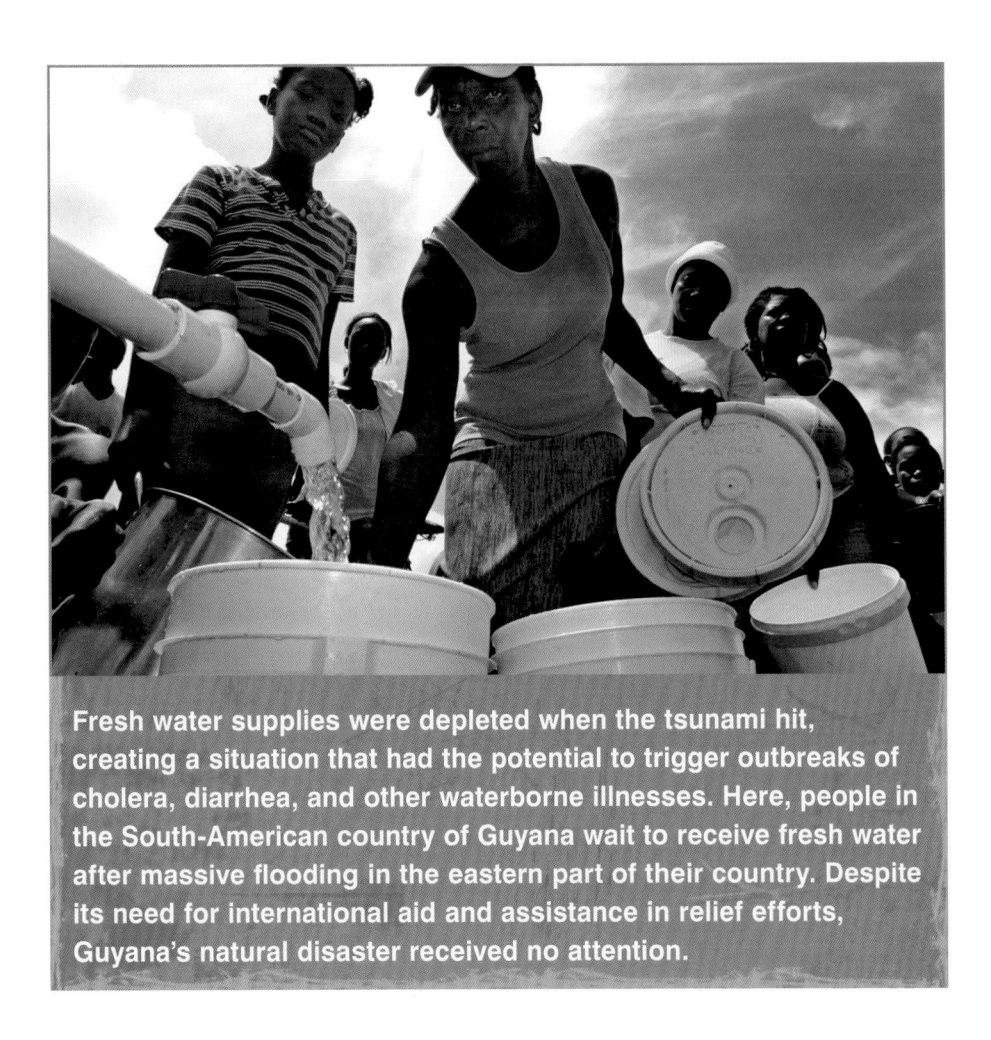

Fresh water supplies were depleted when the tsunami hit, creating a situation that had the potential to trigger outbreaks of cholera, diarrhea, and other waterborne illnesses. Here, people in the South-American country of Guyana wait to receive fresh water after massive flooding in the eastern part of their country. Despite its need for international aid and assistance in relief efforts, Guyana's natural disaster received no attention.

Britain agreed to donate at least a day's salary to buy emergency medicines. Their donations were matched by Generics, a British drug firm.

Nevertheless, not all donations of drugs and vaccines were welcome. Some pharmacies and manufacturers shipped medicines that had been returned by the original purchaser or others that were beyond their expiration date. Others donated drugs that were not needed in the affected areas. Finally, WHO felt it necessary to issue a statement calling on manufacturers to follow certain guidelines and asking pharmacists and other health professions to donate money instead of medicine.

In some cases, medicine was not only in short supply but did not exist at all. No vaccine exists for malaria, although researchers hope to have one developed by the year 2010. But malaria, at least, could be treated with an array of quinine-based drugs. Such was not the case with dengue fever, which had affected more than 58,000 people in Indonesia in 2004. There is no specific treatment for dengue fever, and at the time of the tsunami, no research was underway to find a vaccine.

In addition to drugs, medical supplies were sorely needed. "The immediate needs, particularly in Indonesia, are for antibiotics, syringes, intravenous lines, catheters, bandages, dressings and surgical tape to respond to the injuries and infections," Project Hope president John Howe was quoted as saying in the book *Tsunami: Hope, Heroes, and Incredible Stories of Survival.*

While getting drugs and medicine to those who needed them was a problem, it was sometimes equally difficult for medical personnel to reach their patients. This was true not only for doctors and nurses in the affected countries but also for those coming in from abroad. Australian surgeon Peter Sharwood took various flights for 15 hours to reach Banda Aceh, but once at the airport, he was unable to get transportation into the city to begin work. In an article in the South African newspaper *Mail & Guardian*, the frustrated Sharwood said, "People need to be treated now ... Those who had life-threatening injuries to start with have probably already died."

As quickly as they could, however, teams of medical personnel spread throughout the area, providing treatment and

Volunteer Nurses

As a former chief of the U.S. Army Nurse Corps, William Bester thought he had seen almost everything. That was before the retired general, now a member of the nursing faculty at the University of Texas, was recruited to lead a mercy mission to Indonesia in the wake of the tsunami.

"The devastation reminded me of photographs I had seen of Hiroshima [the Japanese city hit with the first atomic bomb in 1945]," he said in an article on the University of Texas Web site. "You can't fully describe absolute ruin in words."

Another team member, Texas nursing graduate student Ronda Schultz, said, "It looked like I would imagine another planet would look."

The two nurses were part of a combined mission of Project Hope, a nonprofit relief organization, and the U.S. Navy. Project Hope recruited doctors and nurses, who went to Indonesia and provided health care using the facilities of the U.S.S. *Mercy*, a U.S. Navy hospital ship. It was the first such joint civilian-military mission and "all in all, it was a great success," Bester said.

The team consisted of 200 medical professionals, who alternated in six-week rotations. Many of those in the first rotation volunteered to remain for the second, including Schultz. "I was blessed to have been able to participate in this mission. I stayed for both rotations and worked with just about every patient who came on the ship."

helping local officials with vaccination programs. The International Medical Corps, a nonprofit agency headquartered in California, dispatched several teams, one of which provided around-the-clock emergency room staffing in Banda Aceh. Also in the Indonesian city was an Australian team that performed up to 30 major operations each day.

CRITICIZING THE WORLD HEALTH ORGANIZATION

As more and more help arrived—doctors, nurses, drugs, vaccines, equipment—many people began to reexamine WHO's initial assessment that disease could claim as many lives as had the tsunami. "It's impossible to make a prediction like that," Columbia University's Dr. Stephen Morse told ABC News. And the same news account quoted Dr. Duane Gubler of the University of Hawaii as saying, "I'm not sure where the gloom and doom stories of massive epidemics killing more people than the tsunami came from, but they are off the mark."

One critic went so far as to claim that WHO might have deliberately overstated the threat. In an article on the Indonesia Relief Web site, Dr. Wim Van Damme of the Institute of Tropical Medicine in Antwerp, Belgium, said, "There was in fact no danger at all of a huge epidemic, but there was a kind of collective sensationalism. It's also a good way of raising resources, and that's, I think, what happened and it's very disappointing that, indeed, WHO rather sensationalized it."

Faced with such criticism and the lack of any epidemics, WHO's Nabarro began to back away from his earlier prediction. In a *China Daily* article, he said that his comments were made when the tsunami death toll was about 50,000, not 200,000. "With approximately five million people in need of relief, a potential death total of 50,000 due to diarrhea and disease is not at all unreasonable," he said.

It might have been, some said, that the news media's widespread reporting and expansion of Nabarro's prediction of disaster was the very thing that prevented it from occurring. As Philip Maher of the aid group World Vision said in a Yahoo! India News story, "After disasters like this, there are often predictions that there is going to be a second wave of diseases and in most cases it doesn't happen. Maybe the reason is because there is a warning flare that goes up, and everyone kicks into action."

Nabarro agreed, telling the BBC, "It's the first time I've seen the international community organise itself so well." He added, however, that "it's very important that people realize that it could have been amazingly terrible."

MENTAL PROBLEMS

But while tsunami survivors may not have encountered physical consequences to the extent predicted, they nevertheless faced a medical emergency equally as serious—severe mental problems suffered as a result of having witnessed so much death and destruction. "There are areas where everybody knew someone who lost everything or who had one or more family members disappear," Dr. Pau Perez Sales said in a World Health Organization bulletin. "The tsunami will be a landmark in the memory of many communities."

The memory was particularly hard to erase because of the evidence that met people's eyes in the days following the disaster. Piled-up, unburied bodies were grim reminders to survivors of what had happened to friends and relatives. Burying the bodies in mass graves only made the problem worse. Roger Yates of the relief organization Action Aid said in a NewScientist.com article that "if bodies are simply dumped in mass graves relatives never know what happened to their loved ones, which can also cause distress."

The extent of the mental trauma caused by the tsunami was shown in two studies done in Thailand by the United States Centers for Disease Control and Prevention. The first study involved children and found that of the approximately

20,000 children directly affected by the tsunami, between 11 and 13 percent showed signs of post-traumatic stress disorder (PTSD). The rate was much the same in a follow-up study nine months after the tsunami. A similar study of Thai adults showed that 37 percent of adults displaced by the disaster had symptoms of either PTSD or anxiety.

Curiously, the reported incidence of psychological trauma was much less in Indonesia, the country that suffered the most from the tsunami. A study published by the University of Wisconsin showed that 24 percent of patients surveyed in a Red Cross hospital showed signs of depression, but only two patients were diagnosed with a mental-health problem. This

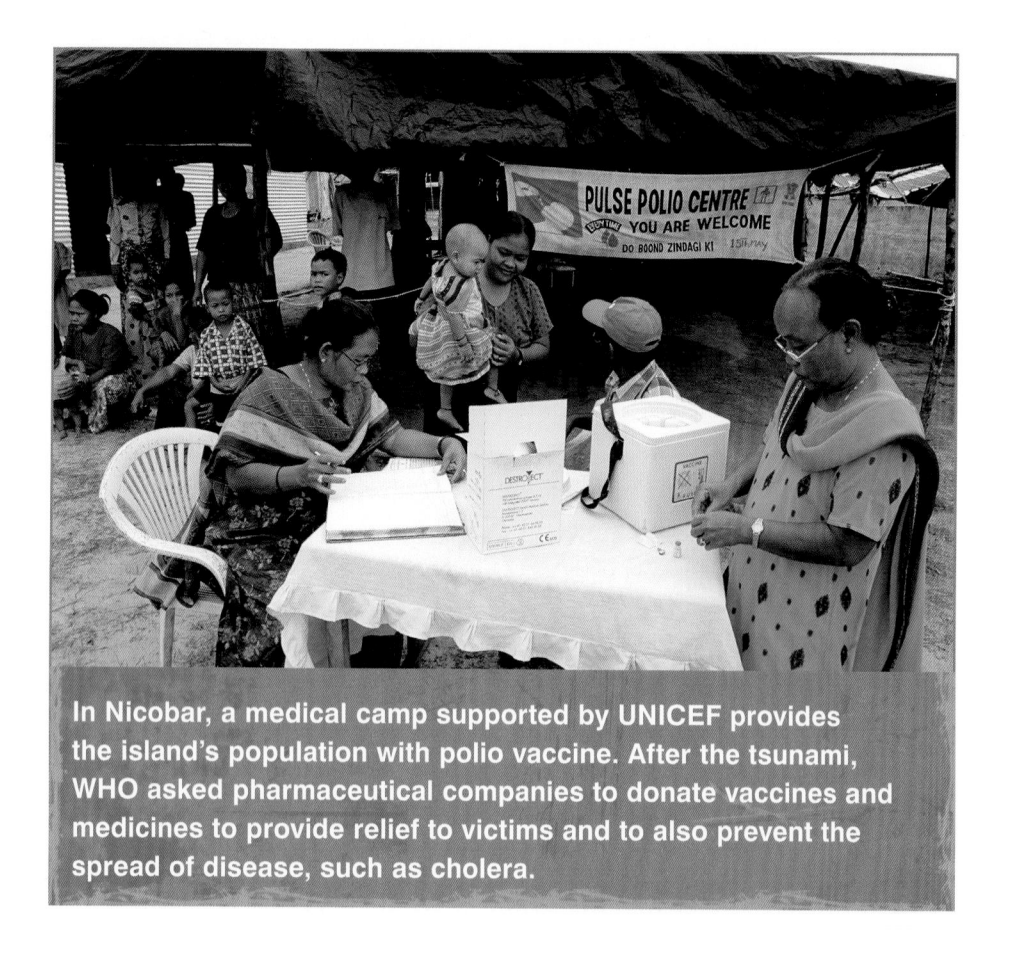

In Nicobar, a medical camp supported by UNICEF provides the island's population with polio vaccine. After the tsunami, WHO asked pharmaceutical companies to donate vaccines and medicines to provide relief to victims and to also prevent the spread of disease, such as cholera.

might have been, the study report said, a cultural issue: "The culture in Aceh usually does not endorse open displays of emotion and grief, so perhaps doctors were not asking openly about mental health symptoms."

Some of the areas most affected were no more ready to deal with psychological problems than they were with physical trauma. Indonesia's Aceh Province had three psychiatrists serving a population of 4.5 million. And Andrew Dawson, a social worker in Sri Lanka, told the *Australian* newspaper, "There are more Sri Lankan psychiatrists in London than there are in Sri Lanka."

Indeed, there was only one psychiatrist, Mahesan Ganesan, on Sri Lanka's eastern coast, an area of 1.3 million people, and he was far too busy after the tsunami distributing medicine and coordinating treatment efforts to even begin to deal with stress disorders. "To talk about psychological needs when you've got thousands of people using one toilet in a refugee camp—it's absurd," Ganesan told the *Washington Post*. "It's not what a doctor should do."

Emotional scars would remain with the tsunami survivors, however, long after other wounds had healed. As time passed, and there was no word of missing relatives, anxiety increased. "There were a lot of families that were in denial because the bodies were not found," Ganesan told the Australian Broadcasting Corporation. "The problem is when the body is not found, then the denial stays for months and sometimes years. What do you do? Do you think the child is dead or alive? You want the child to be alive but, at the same time, you know to some extent they are not. . . . It's a very difficult dilemma."

SURVIVORS' GUILT

Many survivors, experts said, could not understand why they had been spared when so many friends and family members had been lost. "They have the guilt of surviving when others did not," Father Paul Satkunanyagam, a Sri Lankan psychologist, told the *Times*. "Many of these people are very religious and they question whether God is punishing them."

An assessment by a team from Doctors Without Borders, published by the United States National Institute of Health, found much the same thing in Indonesia. "Without exception, the [Muslim] people we spoke with during the assessment understood the tsunami as a punishment or a warning from Allah for being 'immoral,'" the authors wrote. "Many believe that the earth will continue to shake until all the dead are buried."

Even people who did not lose family members were affected, particularly people who had lost their livelihood (such as fishermen whose boats had been destroyed). The Doctors Without Borders report said that while men in Banda Aceh wanted to rebuild their lives, they were frustrated at not being able to do so and feel "great sadness."

Indeed, deaths from the tsunami would continue long after the drownings, long after the last case of cholera or malaria. "They are in despair," Father Satkunanayagam said in the *Times*. "They have lost everything and can see no future. They are losing the will to live."

One such person was Piyawat Suksrikaew. The 18-year-old was found hanging from a pine tree on a beach in Thailand four months after the tsunami. A neighbor told the *Nation* newspaper in Bangkok that, while the boy had been cheerful and well-mannered before the disaster, "after he lost his mother and younger sister, he was depressed and became absent minded. He often talked to himself." Throughout the tsunami region, rates of suicide increased dramatically.

Nevertheless, the overall health situation was such that by February 11 the Environment News Service could report health officials "breathing a sigh of relief." WHO's Nabarro said that, although conditions were right for epidemics, the international response prevented them. "This time we actually got it right," he told the BBC.

But, although the epidemic threat seemed to have passed, there was much more work to be done—in health care and in helping people to rebuild their lives. "The second wave is being averted in most places as we speak," United Nations Emergency Relief Coordinator Jan Egeland said in a report on the UN Web site. "Now the really hard work starts and that is provide a life for the people." That task would involve not only hard work but also a massive outpouring of aid from every corner of the world.

5 Response, Relief, Recovery

Within a week of the tsunami, Kofi Annan, then-secretary-general of the United Nations (UN), had assessed the damage and come to a conclusion. "This is an unprecedented global catastrophe and it requires an unprecedented global response," he said in a statement reported by the *New York Times*. "Over the last few days it has registered deeply in the conscience of the world."

The world heeded Annan's call to duty. Starting in just days and extending for months, a great inpouring of money, supplies, and volunteer labor came from all corners of the globe. The effort was by no means perfect, but it meant the difference between life and death, productivity or poverty, for many thousands of tsunami survivors.

The extent of the disaster was further underscored by United States Secretary of State Colin Powell. After flying by helicopter over Sumatra, the former army general and seasoned combat veteran said in a *Dallas Morning News* article: "I've been in war, and I have been through a number of hurricanes, tornadoes and other relief operations, but I have never seen anything like this."

Jan Egeland, the man who would play perhaps the single largest role in relief efforts, had a similar reaction. Egeland, the United Nations emergency relief coordinator and under-secretary-general for humanitarian affairs, was asleep in his New York City apartment when a phone call gave him the news. Like millions of others, he turned on his television and saw the first pictures of the devastation. "We were not even close to understanding the true enormity of it," he said later in an article in the *Age*. "The initial indication was that a few hundred were affected."

As the extent of the damage slowly became apparent, nations around the world began to offer support. On the day after the tsunami, the European Union gave $4 million and pledged $27 million more. Some individual European countries—Ireland, Spain, Germany, and Belgium—as well as Canada pledged about $1 million each. The United States pledged $15 million.

UNITED STATES, OTHERS "STINGY"

The UN's Egeland was far from satisfied. In a statement reported in the *Washington Times*, he said, "It is beyond me why we are so stingy. Christmastime should remind many Western countries, at least [of] how rich we've become."

The criticism stung, especially in the United States, where many politicians assumed that Egeland's remarks were directed at them. A White House aide, Trent Duffy, told the *Washington Times* that the United States had traditionally led the way in global relief and that "the American people are very giving." Nevertheless, only one day later, the U.S. pledge was increased to $35 million.

Moreover, U.S. president George W. Bush, on Christmas vacation at his Texas ranch, was drawing criticism for having failed to make a public statement. "The president doesn't like the idea of empty gestures," an aide told *Newsweek*, but the

After UN emergency relief coordinator and undersecretary general for humanitarian affairs, Jan Egeland (*above*) said that privileged countries were being too "stingy" in their pledges and monetary donations to the tsunami relief effort, many nations increased their pledges.

next day, Bush appeared before television cameras to express his condolences.

Eventually, the relief effort almost became a competition among countries as to which was the most generous. Between government pledges and private donations, the United States led the way with $2.8 billion, and Australia and Germany donated $1.3 billion each. Other leading donor nations were the United Kingdom ($795 million), Canada ($743 million), the Netherlands ($509 million), Japan ($500 million), Saudi Arabia ($367 million), France ($302 million), and Switzerland ($200 million).

Australia's pledge, however, had to be considered the most generous. Its total of $1.3 billion represented 2.44 percent of the nation's gross national product (GNP), or annual economic production. The United States's GNP percentage equivalent, on the other hand, was 0.26.

The estimated total of donations by governments worldwide was in excess of $10 billion. As the amount grew, Egeland was ecstatic. In an MSNBC story, he said, "Indeed the world is coming together in a manner we have never ever seen before. . . . We are just not able to record all the generous offers, they are coming in so often and they are so big."

Such generosity, however, did not put an end to the grumbling. Except for Saudi Arabia, the only other mostly Muslim Middle-Eastern countries making pledges were the United Arab Emirates, Qatar, and Kuwait, and those pledges totaled $145 million. Some survivors in Muslim nations such as Somalia and Indonesia wondered publicly and angrily why more aid was not forthcoming. Egeland was more diplomatic, saying in a UN media release, "What I have really welcomed is to see that there is now a discussion in several Muslim countries" about giving more.

Over the next few months, it also became evident that promising was one thing but actually giving was another.

Six months after the tsunami, the aid organization Action-Aid International reported that Australia had thus far given only 7 percent of what had been pledged, France 13 percent, Germany 16 percent, and the United States and the European Union 38 percent. Great Britain, on the other hand, had fulfilled 97 percent of its pledge and Japan 100 percent. Also, a full year after the disaster, the *Orlando Sentinel* reported on a UN study showing that some nations, such as China, had not contributed anything despite large pledges.

Presidential Aid

President George W. Bush pledged $350 million from the U.S. government to aid victims of the tsunami, and he also enlisted the help of his two immediate predecessors—his father, George H.W. Bush, and Bill Clinton—in organizing a major private fund-raising initiative. "I have asked two of America's most distinguished private citizens to head a nationwide charitable fund-raising effort," the junior Bush said in an article on the Cable News Network Web site.

President Bush had been criticized during the first few days after the tsunami for pledging $15 million in aid, a sum some called "stingy." The president's father was asked if announcing the private effort was intended to stop the criticism. "That's not what this is about," the elder Bush said in a *Washington Post* article. "It's about saving lives. It's about caring, and the president cares."

By the fall of 2006, the Bush-Clinton Tsunami Fund had raised more than $1 billion, and the former presidents were honored with the 2006 Philadelphia Liberty Medal.

PRIVATE CHARITIES

Governments, meanwhile, were not the only sources of help. Charities said that the increase in donations reminded them of the days following the September 11, 2001, terrorist attacks. The *New York Daily News* reported less than two weeks after the tsunami that the American Red Cross had collected $79 million and the British aid organization Oxfam more than $12 million.

High-profile individuals were at the forefront of the effort. Actress Sandra Bullock donated $1 million, and actor Leonardo DiCaprio was reported to have given a similar amount. DiCaprio had special ties to the affected area, having shot the 2000 film *The Beach* on Thailand's Phi Phi island. Professional athletes also came forward. Some teams took up collections during halftimes. Several professional basketball players, including the Los Angeles Lakers' Kobe Bryant, promised to donate $1,000 for every point he scored in a designated game. He scored 27.

Relief agencies, however, could not wait. Even before the first donations arrived, they began to gear up for what they were beginning to realize would be one of the most massive humanitarian ventures ever undertaken. One of those setting the wheels in motion was Colleen McGinn, an Oxfam worker living in Melbourne, Australia.

McGinn was enjoying tea with a boyfriend at about 6 P.M. when the phone call came from a supervisor, Marlene McIntyre. McIntyre told her there had been an earthquake and tsunami and that her help was needed immediately.

At first, McGinn thought she was the victim of a joke. It had been one year ago to the day that she received a similar call about an earthquake in Iran. "Very funny, Marlene," she was quoted as saying in a *New York Times* article. "Merry Christmas to you, too."

She soon learned it was no joke. She and her Oxfam colleagues worked through the night and into the next day telephoning workers and agencies throughout south and east

A New Start

When World Vision, an international relief agency, offered to help the people of Suak Timah, a village about 240 miles south of Banda Aceh in Indonesia, Maryam Pahang was quick to accept the offer. As a result, she was able to replace her small coffee shop that was swept out to sea by the tsunami.

"I remember it was a very still day and there was no wind blowing. We started to head home and, on the way, an earthquake began shaking the ground and then, suddenly, the earth cracked in two in front of me," she said in an article on the ReliefWeb Internet site.

Shortly afterward, a wave swept Pahang more than a mile inland, where she was able to take refuge in the top of a rubber tree. When she was finally able to return to the village, she found only empty ground on the site where her coffee shop had been.

When World Vision offered assistance, she requested and received a loan to buy some new land. World Vision then built her a small building in which she could reopen her business.

"World Vision agreed to support me with this coffee shop and provided these chairs, tables, the food cabinet and stock like coffee, soft drinks and sugar," Pahang said. "And from the first profits, we were able to buy more stock as you see here."

In less than two years, Pahang and her husband were able to pay off their loan and to upgrade their shop by buying a refrigerator to keep drinks cool.

Asia. Within hours, tons of supplies were being packed into airplanes to be airlifted to Indonesia and Sri Lanka.

A day later, McGinn was on one of those planes. She was a veteran of disasters, having worked with war refugees in Africa, the Middle East, and eastern Europe, but nothing had prepared her for what she found in Sri Lanka. "The destruction was unreal. When I showed up I could smell the bodies and for about a kilometer in from the beach was absolute and total devastation," she said in an article written for a newsletter at Ohio University, where she had earned a degree. "Boats in treetops, huge bridges washed away. One image that stays with me is wandering through the ruins of a Hindu temple, with little bits of broken gods strewn about. And, of course, the people. I met one woman who had lost her four children, husband, and both parents."

McGinn would be joined in the tsunami region by thousands of others—relief agency workers, volunteers, and military personnel. By the second week in January, approximately 13,000 military personnel were in the area along with 17 U.S. Navy vessels, a Coast Guard cutter, and about 90 aircraft, most of them helicopters used to airlift supplies into stricken areas and to evacuate seriously ill or injured people to places where they could receive medical care. Eleven other countries also sent military personnel.

In addition, the UN quickly opened 200 relief centers throughout the region, and medical help began to arrive from the Red Cross and World Health Organization. Oxfam, in addition to providing immediate emergency assistance, concentrated on building temporary housing, repairing and rebuilding water and sanitation facilities, and starting a program designed to restore livelihoods to those deprived of work. By July, Oxfam had spent about $65 million in the region and was planning a three-year reconstruction program that would cost more than $250 million.

SELF-HELP

The affected countries did not depend solely on outside help. Even Indonesia, which had been hit the hardest and had the economy least able to deal with the damage, was managing to deal with some of the short-term problems. Within a week of the tsunami, the Indonesian government had managed to get bulldozers and other heavy equipment into hard-to-reach areas to assist in clearing rubble. And a government relief official reported that 40 percent of Banda Aceh's electricity had been restored as well as complete cellular telephone service. Land-line telephones were still out because most of the telephone company's repair employees had been killed.

Elephants were used in Thailand to help with the cleanup *(above)*. Before the earthquake, they had run for higher ground, saving people along the way.

Thailand was able to mount a more effective response. On the same day as the tsunami hit, the government established a relief collaboration center in Phuket headed by Thai Minister of the Interior Kongsak Wanthana. Wanthana assigned deputy ministers to oversee affected provinces and to coordinate such activities as victim identification, getting foreign tourists back home, and distribution of supplies. The government also aided tourists by setting up a 24-hour facility for telephoning relatives and by making donations of cash and clothing to those who had lost everything.

Although Thailand would receive more than $30 million in outside relief funds from the UN and other sources, the Thais shouldered most of the financial load and made no appeal for foreign assistance. The government tapped the budgets of 13 departments plus the prime minister's office for an estimated $1 billion. A large segment of the Thai military was also mobilized and sent to the area.

India, likewise, assumed most of the burden for relief and reconstruction. The Indian government, in fact, announced it would bear the entire cost, estimated at $1.6 billion.

THE CASTE QUESTION

The relief effort in India, however, would soon come under fire from some of its citizens. A *Washington Post* article told of a farm worker, Muthu Vellaithevan, who said he and others from his village were expelled from a refugee shelter because they were Dalits, members of what was once known as the "untouchable" caste. "They [other Indians] did not want to be under the same roof with us," Vellaithevan said. "We were forced to leave. Our homes were destroyed and our children were hungry. Where could we go?"

The caste system, a rigid separation of people into social levels, has been officially outlawed in India for decades but still lingers in rural areas. The Dalits, at the lowest end of the system, are considered unclean by others. Although the Indian government claimed there was no caste discrimination in aid distribution, others were not so sure. "In many relief camps the government is not giving them aid, saying the dalits have not been affected by the tsunamis," Ravi Chandran of the nongovernmental Village Development Society said in a Deutsche Presse-Agentur article. "We sent a petition two days back to the police and state government to speed up aid for the dalits because they were not receiving anything. There has been no response."

The Dalits' problems were just one example of the extent to which cultural and political issues interfered with relief efforts. In Indonesia, for instance, the province of Aceh had been trying for 30 years to establish its independence. Martial law had been established in 2002, and foreign aid workers were barred from the area. The tsunami forced the central government to relax the ban, but it said all foreigners had to leave Aceh by the end of March, a deadline ultimately extended.

The relief efforts did not entirely set aside internal political differences. Within two weeks after the tsunami, the Indonesian government reported that some of its soldiers had been fired on by rebel guerrillas. The Free Aceh movement, in turn, accused the government of trying to take advantage of the situation to increase its military presence.

Much the same situation existed in Sri Lanka, where the resistance group known as the Tamil Tigers had been trying to establish an independent state. After the tsunami, the Tamil Tigers accused the Sri Lankan government of deliberately withholding aid to areas under their control. The two sides eventually worked out an agreement to share responsibility for aid distribution, but trouble continued when the Tigers were accused of recruiting orphaned children as soldiers.

THE "CORE GROUP"

Political infighting also took place on a more global scale. At an international meeting aimed at coordinating aid, a self-proclaimed "core group" was formed by the United States, India, Australia, and Japan. Critics immediately complained that the underlying intent of the core group was to bypass the United Nations, freeze China out of the process, and allow India to create stronger ties with the United States and Japan.

Oxfam protested the move, its East Asia regional director, Ashvin Dayal, saying in a press release, "There is a risk of chaos in the aid response in Indonesia. So far, the United Nations is ensuring the relief aid and workers are starting to get through to Aceh, where the worst suffering is. We now need the best assessments of need, and the proper allocation of responsibilities between the agencies to maximize the benefits of the aid that is given. Only the United Nations can do this, with the Government of Indonesia. The US-led core group must come under the umbrella of the United Nations to be effective."

Political problems were not the only ones plaguing the relief effort. The enormity of the task led to waste and to delays in getting aid and supplies to those needing them most. Some of the delays could not be avoided, since transportation into many areas had been disrupted, but some were the result of almost bizarre accidents. In one case, a water buffalo managed to wander onto the runway of the Banda Aceh airport, where it was struck by a landing plane loaded with supplies. The buffalo was killed, and the damage to the airplane closed the airport for 17 hours, during which time other aircraft bringing aid could not land.

During times when Banda Aceh's airport was either out of commission or backed up, aircraft were diverted to Medan, 280 miles to the south. Conditions there, however, were little better. The pilot of a Belgian Air Force plane told the *London Times* that the unloading of his plane took six hours instead of the usual 45 minutes. The problem was that mechanized loaders were busy elsewhere, and all of his six-ton cargo had to be unloaded by hand. "Time is money," he said, "but time is also life."

Moreover, the supplies, once unloaded, often sat piled up for days or weeks because there was no way to transport them. As Indonesian Air Force General Chappy Hakim told the *Guardian,* "The bottleneck is in the distribution once the aid gets here. We need more trucks to deliver the supplies and more helicopters."

But transportation, if available, was often uncertain. Even when highways were open, there was a danger that supplies would not get through. John Budd of UNICEF reported in the *London Times* that "there are already reports of people holding up cars and vehicles. There's certainly a security problem on the road along that [Indonesian] coast."

HAPHAZARD DELIVERIES

Even when supplies managed to arrive at a destination, delivery was sometimes haphazard. A relief worker in Sri Lanka told *TIME* that the distribution of food was "completely chaotic. Whoever runs up to the truck and grabs, gets food. The workers have no idea who actually needs aid." And in Banda Aceh, drivers fearful of their vehicles being overwhelmed simply dumped their food on the ground without stopping. Then, one man told the *London Times,* "the fastest get the food, the strong one wins. The elderly and the injured don't get anything. We feel like dogs."

Sometimes the supplies reaching stricken areas were not what was really needed. In India, government relief workers took large amounts of warm clothing to people who were sweltering under the tropical Sun. Villagers stacked the unwanted garments on roadsides and burned them.

At times, the problem was not the wrong supplies, but the wrong people. Even doctors, whose skills were desperately needed, could get in the way. Sri Lankan psychiatrist Mahesan Ganesan told the *Washington Post* about a Korean medical team that parachuted into the remote town of Batticaola. No one on the team spoke a local language, and only one spoke English.

Damaged roadways and backed up airports hampered efforts to meet the supply needs of the tsunami victims in more remote areas. Regions in Indonesia and Sri Lanka required the national governments to work with rebel forces and foreign-aid groups to provide support. Here, Red Cross workers use boats to deliver supplies to the remote island of Gizo in the Solomon Islands.

The only way for the group to communicate with their patients was through the one local person who also spoke English.

The Koreans had brought no medicine with them and had to rely on local supplies, the labels on which they could not read. One doctor, thinking he was giving a vitamin syrup to children, actually was having them drink calamine lotion intended as an external treatment for skin inflammations. "At least we found out it won't kill you," Ganesan laughed.

Other people, whether they had good intentions or not, only got in the way. In India, several leading politicians considered it absolutely necessary to visit the disaster zone in person and accompanied by television crews. Such visits contributed little and instead hampered the effort by drawing hundreds of police officers away from relief duties to security. Another problem reported in India was that of "disaster tourists," amateurs who arrived in the country with supplies but with no idea as to which supplies were needed or what to do with them.

SLOW RECOVERY

Eventually, however, the bottlenecks began to unclog, political squabbles to abate, and the relief effort speeded up. In India, only days after the tsunami, fishing boats took to the sea once more. "The tsunami changed these waters," Vivek Harinarain, a government official told the BBC. "Now there are huge catches waiting for us."

In Banda Aceh, as electric power and sanitation facilities were restored, the city began to come back to life. Schools reopened, as did shops and markets. Street vendors like Eddy Yahya, a coconut seller, were back in business. "It's still difficult to get enough supplies here," he told the *Washington Post*, "but more are coming."

In Thailand, the tourist industry began to recover, but it was a slow process. In Phuket, two years after the tsunami, about 20 percent of the more than 500 hotels were still inoperable. But, although the hotels were open, fewer guests came. A year after the disaster, room occupancy was only 50 percent of what it had been the previous year. While many hotels could afford to operate at a loss, waiting on business to pick up, the same was not true for many others dependent on tourism. Numerous owners of restaurants and small shops went out of business.

Still, the United Nations's Egeland was able to give a generally upbeat report when he appeared on the CNN program *American Morning* on the first anniversary of the tsunami: "I think we can sum up the whole response to the tragedy in one sentence," he said. "It went better as a relief effort than we feared, and it has gone slower as a recovery effort than we had initially hoped. . . . Too many have this one-year anniversary today in the same tents as they got in the first few weeks. Most of them, however, will be in real homes, much better than they had before the tsunami, before the second anniversary."

There was at least one place, however, where the international relief effort could not be called a success because it never began. The people of Sentinel, one of the Andaman and Nicobar islands, live much the same way as did their ancestors thousands of years ago—hunting and fishing, living in straw huts—and fiercely resisting any outside interference. Two days after the tsunami, an Indian helicopter approach the island to check on the Sentinelese. As it approached the beach, a lone Sentinelese man emerged from the jungle, raised his bow, and shot an arrow at the offending machine. It was a signal that his people wanted to be left alone—a signal the government of India honored.

6 The Next Tsunami

Even as survivors of the Indian Ocean tsunami began picking up the pieces of their property and lives, scientists and governments around the world were asking themselves three questions: When and where would the next tsunami hit? How could those in its path receive more warning? How might those in danger areas prepare themselves or take immediate action?

The short answer to the first question is that no one knows the time and place of the next tsunami. While science can pinpoint areas where tsunamis are likely to occur and estimate that likelihood, any notion of when one might occur is guesswork. "If anyone tells you they know, they're pulling your leg," Rob McCaffrey, a geophysics professor at Rensselaer Polytechnic Institute, said in an Associated Press article carried on the MSNBC Web site.

Franz Kessler, an explorer for oil and gas who also has taught deepwater geology, put it another way. In an article on the Authors' Den Web site, he compared undersea tectonic forces to a loaded gun: "The bullet is loaded, and the spring is being squeezed. A gentle touch on the trigger—spontaneous energy is released."

The question about the next tsunami, scientists say, is not if, but when. Their ideas of when, however, vary widely. Speaking of the Indian Ocean, geologist Kerry Sieh, in a *Bangkok Post* article carried on a water-safety Web site, said, "I'd be surprised if it were delayed much beyond 30 years." A British official, Gareth Thomas, told the *London Times* he looked for an Indian Ocean tsunami "at some point in the next 50 years." But Phil Cummins, senior analyst at Geoscience Australia monitoring organization, in a NewsFox article, was less certain. "It could happen any time," he said. "It could take another 20 to 50 years, or another 200 years."

The problem with predicting when a tsunami might occur, said Roger Bilham of the University of Colorado in the Associated Press/MSNBC.com article, is that the data scientists need to make such a prediction—the exact extent of tectonic forces and the relationship of plates to one another—are out of reach. He compared it to predicting when a ripe apple might fall from a tree. "Earthquake prediction is much more difficult than that, because you don't even see the apple."

RISKS EVERYWHERE

Enough is known about plate tectonics and other undersea geology, however, for scientists to answer the "where" question—and the answers are surprising. The most likely candidates—the areas around the Indian Ocean and Pacific Rim—are by no means the only ones at risk.

The Atlantic Ocean, for instance, is not immune. Although it lacks the dramatic tectonic plate activity of the Pacific, it does have volcanoes—another possible cause of tsunamis. One volcano, in particular, has drawn the attention of scientists.

In 1949, a volcano named Cumbre Vieja on the island of La Palma in the Canary Island group off the northwestern coast of Africa erupted. A large piece of the mountain—about 130 cubic miles—was shaken loose and is presently perched precariously on the western mountainside, slipping into the ocean a few inches at a time. Another eruption, however, could send it crashing down all at once, creating an enormous wave.

Bill McGuire of University College London estimates that the initial waves will be as high as 300 feet, swamping most of the Canary Islands and sweeping far inland on the western coast of Africa. Secondary waves as high as 150 feet would speed across the Atlantic, hitting the Caribbean islands and the eastern seaboards of the United States and Canada. Such waves, McGuire said on *NOVA*, would "expend the same energy for every [300 feet] of coastline as was generated by the collapse of the Twin Towers [in the September 11, 2001, terrorist attack].

Redrawing the Map

The Indian Ocean earthquake and tsunami were so powerful that they changed the Earth's surface. An article on *National Geographic*'s Web site told of reports of entire islands that had vanished, coastlines that had been altered, and ocean floor that had been restructured in places that posed a danger to shipping.

To measure such changes and to help in relief operations, David Skole and his team from the Center for Global Change and Earth Observations at Michigan State University used high-density satellite imagery. "The signature of the damage is pretty striking," Skole said, "[We're seeing] significant coastline erosion and new islands that were once connected to the coastline."

It is the erosion, said Chris Anreasen of the National Geospatial-Intelligence Agency in Maryland, that poses potential

And that's for thousands of [miles] all the way down the east coast." The result: coastal cities from Miami to Boston would suffer great destruction.

Scientists are monitoring volcanic activity on La Palma, but not to the extent McGuire believes necessary. There are some seismometers on the island but—in McGuire's opinion—too few. In an article in the *Guardian* he said, "It's really a worrying situation. It will almost certainly go during an eruption [and] we may not get the notice we need."

McGuire said that an adequate system with more seismometers and satellite observation would cost a few hundred

hazards to shipping. "That sediment had to go somewhere, so I'd expect shoaling [shallow water] in channels and areas where vessels typically try to navigate. We have no idea what that impact is right now."

With satellites unable to gauge the extent of change to shipping lanes and harbors, science has had to get more firsthand information. The U.S. Navy sent one of its coastal survey ships, the U.S.S. *John McDonnel*, to the Strait of Malacca that separates Sumatra from the Malay Peninsula. There, it probed approaches to harbors with onboard sonar.

"We don't know the shape that the channels, approaches, and harbors are in, based on debris," said Captain Jeffrey Best of the Naval Oceanographic Office. "There could be buildings, cars, or all kinds of things blocking those approaches. Our guys need to make sure that it's safe so that we can get the big relief ships in there."

thousand dollars, far less than the damage that might be averted. He is not hopeful, however, that such a system will be put in place. "The US government must be aware of the La Palma threat [but] they're not taking it seriously. Governments change every four to five years and generally they're not interested in these things," he told the *Guardian*.

LANDSLIDES

Undersea landslides are yet another possible trigger of tsunamis, one that poses threats to several coastal cities. Particularly at risk are cities that are built on or near massive layers of sediment put down by major rivers. New Orleans, Louisiana, for instance is built on a thick bed of sediment put down over thousands of years by the Mississippi River. Geologists have shown that some river deltas have collapsed in the past and warn that such a collapse today could well produce a tsunami that would threaten cities all along the Gulf of Mexico. Likewise, large portions of the Nile River delta are unstable, and a landslide there could send a tsunami toward such cities as Rome, Venice, and Athens.

And, just because the Indian Ocean experienced an earthquake and tsunami in 2004 does not mean it could not happen sometime in the near future. The earthquake did not totally eliminate the pressure between plates; rather, it shifted much of it northward. Should another quake of the same size (admittedly a small possibility) hit the same fault line, damage to Thailand and Malaysia could be worse than before.

One reason that another monster earthquake along the same line is unlikely is that smaller quakes have continued to hit the area—one measuring 8.7 in March 2005 and another measuring 6.9 in May. Such smaller quakes, although they do localized damage, serve to partially relieve the pressure.

"The more small-scale earthquakes that occur in that region, the better. But that doesn't mean that somewhere else along that fault zone, you won't get a similar buildup of pressure,"

Professor Ray Cas of Monash University in Melbourne, Australia, said in an article carried on the NewsFox press distribution service. "It's in the zones where there are known active faults, and where there has been little significant earthquake activity for some time, that there needs to be a concern."

The most likely site of the next major tsunami, however, is the area of the world with the most history of such phenomena—the Pacific Ocean. In his AuthorsDen.com article, Kessler describes the ocean as "quivering with seismic life."

THE CASCADIA ZONE

Of particular concern to residents of the western United States and Canada is the Pacific Plate Boundary stretching from California to Alaska. A section of the boundary, the Cascadia Subduction Zone that extends from northern California to Vancouver, needs watching, especially since pressure has built up for hundreds of years. Geologic research has shown that this fault line has experienced 19 large earthquakes over the past 10,000 years, averaging one every 500 years. The last such quake occurred 300 years ago.

"There's really no difference at all between the Pacific Northwest and Sumatra," Oregon State University marine geologist Chris Goldfinger said on *NOVA*. "We're now essentially in the same position Sumatra was on Christmas Day, where we know there's a subduction zone there. We know how long it was since the last one. We know quite a bit about all the previous events going back 10,000 years. The only thing we don't know is what day the next event is going to happen."

Both scientists and government leaders hope that that day, whenever and wherever it arrives, will be less deadly because of improved warning systems. The March 2005 Indian Ocean earthquake, although not as destructive as the one the previous December, served as a wake-up call. "Here we go again," said Brigadier General David L. Johnson, director of the National Weather Service in an article on the Web site of the

National Oceanic and Atmospheric Administration (NOAA). "We knew quickly about the earthquake, its approximate magnitude and location, yet it took hours to determine if, in fact, it created a tsunami."

Johnson added that, had a worldwide system been in place—one using deep-ocean assessment and recording of tsunami (DART) technology, an accurate measurement could have been made within an hour and "the warning message would probably have been canceled."

SCIENTIFIC INACTION

A worldwide system, of course, or even one in the Indian Ocean did not exist at the time of the 2004 tsunami, but it was not because no one understood the danger. Such a system had been discussed for years but with no action. The International Coordination Group for the Tsunami Warning System in the Pacific proposed expansion into the Indian Ocean in 1997, but nothing was done.

Then, in 2003, Phil Cummins, an Australian seismologist, pleaded with the organization at a meeting in New Zealand, citing both geological evidence and historical records of past tsunamis in the Indian Ocean. The only result was that the group passed a resolution calling for, as quoted in a *New York Times* article, "a sessional working group to prepare a recommendation to establish an intersessional working group that will study the establishment of a regional warning system for the Southwest Pacific and Indian Ocean."

Cummins did not give up. He prepared a computer model illustrating the destruction that would be caused by a tsunami originating off Sumatra. No one paid much attention, at least not until after December 26, 2004. Only then did the international community get serious about bringing DART technology to the Indian Ocean.

The DART system uses seismographs on the ocean floor to record earthquakes and, if the quake is 6.5 or greater, to relay

Hoping to prevent another disaster, a tsunami warning system has been implemented on both sides of the United States, as well as the Indian Ocean. Above, the DART deep-ocean sensor is installed as part of an alert system that will allow scientists to gauge data and issue warnings to coastlines when potential giant waves are on their way.

information as to the possible speed and direction of waves to computers such as the ones at the Pacific Tsunami Warning Center in Hawaii. At the same time, buoys on the surface record wave motion and relay similar information. Using both sources, scientists can generate computer models of where the tsunami will strike and with what force.

EXPANDING DART

The United States is in the process of expanding the DART system, adding 32 new buoys to increase surveillance in the Pacific and to add warning systems in the Atlantic and Caribbean. Meanwhile, the first steps have been taken to install a similar system in the Indian Ocean. In August 2005, the United Nations Educational, Scientific and Cultural Organization (UNESCO) held a meeting at which a system of 15 to 28 buoys were approved.

At the meeting, the United States made a two-year, $16.6 million commitment of money and expertise that included the financing and launching of the two buoys, the first of which was launched on December 1, 2006. A U.S. State Department news article reported that the American ambassador to Thailand, Ralph Boyce, said prior to the launch that the buoy would provide "real-time tsunami detection data [to be] freely shared on international telecommunications networks for all countries to receive." A ship then sailed from Phuket to the spot midway between Thailand and Sri Lanka where the buoy was to be positioned.

The second buoy was scheduled to be launched in April 2007 with others to follow. The cost of making the full program operational is estimated at $200 million, far less than the damage done by the tsunami.

DART, however, is not the last word in tsunami alert technology. Japan, which lies in the immediate region of major fault lines, has recognized the importance of issuing warnings within minutes instead of hours and has taken DART technology a step further. In addition to 80 buoys in waters surrounding the islands, there are more than 200 other land-based sensors. The extent and sophistication of the system enable the Japanese to analyze the threat posed by any earthquake and to issue an alert within three minutes. Such alerts can be relayed over radio and television almost instantly.

Had such a system been in place off the coast of Sumatra, even the people of Banda Aceh might have had at least a few minutes to head for higher ground. But, although the Indonesian government was aware of the need for a system, it could

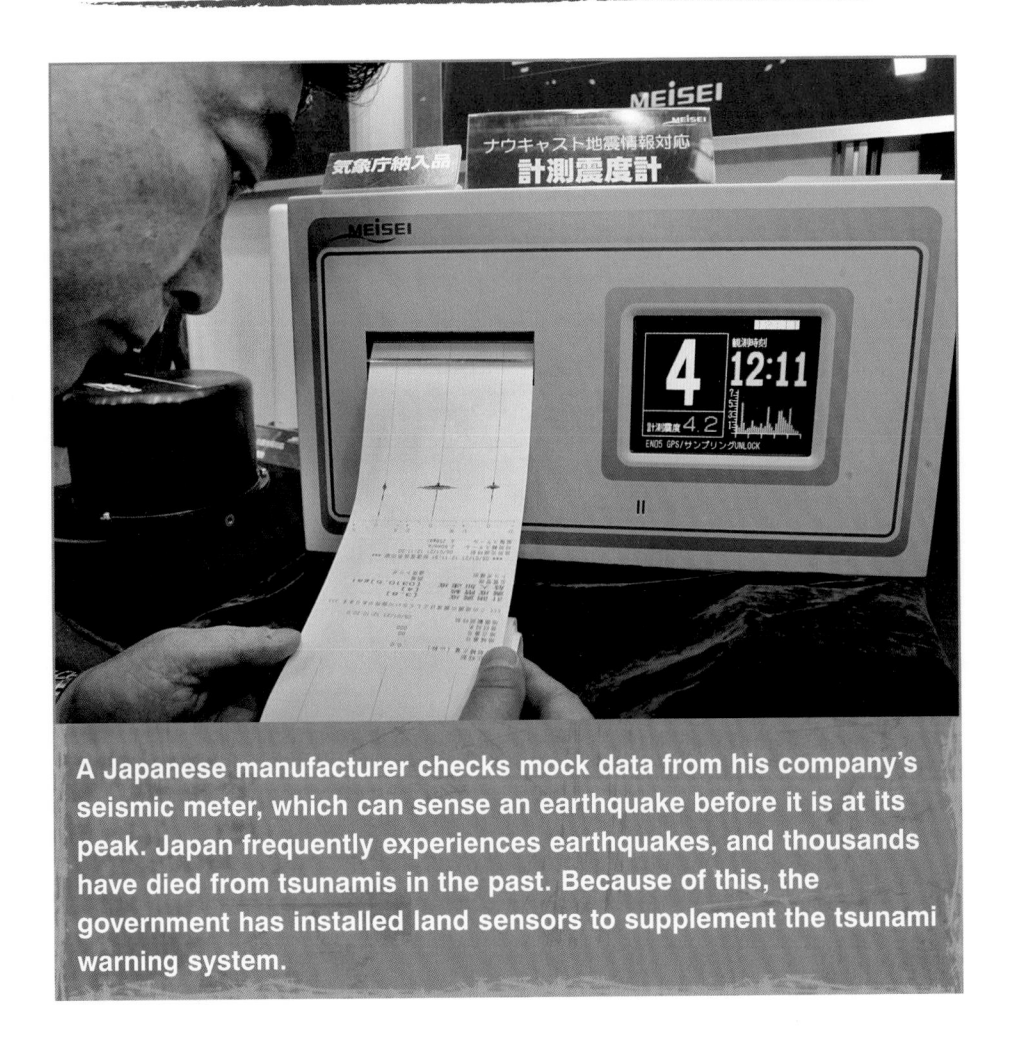

A Japanese manufacturer checks mock data from his company's seismic meter, which can sense an earthquake before it is at its peak. Japan frequently experiences earthquakes, and thousands have died from tsunamis in the past. Because of this, the government has installed land sensors to supplement the tsunami warning system.

not meet the cost. "The instruments are very expensive and we don't have the money to buy them," one official told the *London Times*. Japan spends about $20 million annually just to maintain its network.

SATELLITE TECHNOLOGY

A potentially less expensive and more comprehensive tsunami warning system might be possible with satellites. The 2004 tsunami was observed by satellites, but five hours were needed to process the information. Better data might be available from

Model Proved Correct

Among the scientists most interested in how and where the Indian Ocean tsunami struck was Philip Liu of Cornell University in New York. Liu and a team of researchers had developed a computer model they hoped would quickly predict from an earthquake whether or not it would start a tsunami and how the tsunami would develop.

After the tsunami, Liu went to the Indian Ocean to see how well his computer model had done. It had proved to give correct information, predicting what kind of waves and of what size would strike neighboring countries.

Liu's model, for instance, showed that, when the earthquake occurred, the ocean floor rose upward in one section and sank in another. This displacement of water sent a wave in one direction where the seabed rose and a trough in the opposite direction where the ocean floor had collapsed. This was the reason, Liu said in an article on the Planet Ark Web site, that "positive" waves (surges of water that appeared without warning) hit some areas, and "negative" waves (those that caused water to recede from the shore in advance of the wave) hit others.

The model proved to be correct in other respects as well. It had shown waves wrapping almost completely around the island nation of Sri Lanka. "You would think the [Colombo] region was protected," Liu said of the city on the side of the island opposite from the earthquake site, "but Colombo actually was affected."

Liu hopes that his computer modeling program can someday be made a part of existing tsunami warning systems.

the *Jason 2* satellites due to be launched in 2008 by NOAA and a partnership of European nations.

Yet another space-age possibility for tsunami detection is the Global Navigation Satellite System Reflections (GNSS-R) system that maps the oceans' surfaces using radar. Such a system, Spanish-based scientist François Soulat writes, could record more than 160 10-second measurements within 10 minutes after detecting an abnormal wave and relay information, including speed and direction, to computers on the ground.

The most sophisticated detection system is of little use, however, if the information cannot be transmitted to the people in harm's way. "Putting in the sensors is the easy part," Harley Benz of the U.S. Geological Survey said in a *Christian Science Monitor* article. "The difficult part would be coordination between emergency response agencies in the region."

Curt Barrett, who directs the Indian Ocean project for NOAA, agreed, saying in an article on the State Department's Web site that any system must be "end to end." "Once the warning goes out, people have to know what to do," he said in a *Bangkok Post* article. "All of this information is useless if it doesn't get to the person down on the beach."

Several items in addition to technology are crucial to an effective end-to-end warning system. First, the information must go to a central authority charged with the responsibility of passing it along to citizens. Part of the problem with the 2004 tsunami was that scientists in Hawaii had no idea of whom to call in Indonesia or Sri Lanka.

Second, the central authority must be willing to make hard decisions and to make them quickly. The DART system is far from perfect. Several coastal evacuations in Hawaii, each involving considerable expense and disruption of lives, came as a result of false alarms. Governments must be willing to take that risk.

Third, governments will need to establish some sort of communication network. Some areas have begun setting up

Two years after the tsunami, tourism rebounded in Thailand as coastal communities continue to slowly rebuild. Above, vacationers lounge on the beach beside a tsunami warning tower.

sirens on beaches to sound warnings. Others have established procedures for using radio and television to spread the word. Another possibility is a system that would sent SMS or text messages to cell phones registered to receive them.

Additional elements in a successful system would be a plan of action and an educational program to teach people what actions they should take. Suggestions include providing accessible and clearly marked evacuation routes, strengthening bridges, establishing stronger building codes in vulnerable areas, and even building tsunami-proof towers.

All such measures would be expensive, especially for poorer countries such as Indonesia, but at least one expert, American geologist Kerry Sieh, thinks more funds should be spent on safety measures and less on technology. "You have an earthquake and it last for five minutes. It is shaking so heavily you can't walk. Why do you need a warning? Haven't you got one already?" he said in a *Bangkok Post* article. "It [a warning system] is not just a waste of money, it is a distraction: It gives people a false sense of security."

One of the most dangerous aspects of the next tsunami, then, is that people will have forgotten the last one. While a sense of security may be a long time coming to the areas devastated in 2004, it is a possible consequence of human nature that memories will fade and that governments will find other, more immediate, priorities. To do so, according to Professor Philip Stott of the University of London, is to invite a similar disaster. In an article in the *London Times* he writes, "We forget, at our peril, the innate restlessness of our planet."

Chronology

2004   **December 26:** Massive earthquake off coast of Sumatra sends tsunami in all directions across Indian Ocean.

December 27: United Nations begins mobilizing relief effort; United States pledges $15 million in aid; United Nations's Jan Egeland calls aid pledges of Western countries "stingy."

December 28: Death toll estimated at 60,000.

December 29: Death toll rises above 100,000.

Timeline

December 26
Massive earthquake off coast of Sumatra sends tsunami in all directions across Indian Ocean.

December 31
Death toll hits 150,000; United States increases aid pledge from $15 million to $350 million.

2004

2005

December 27
United Nations begins mobilizing relief effort; United States pledges $15 million in aid; United Nations's Jan Egeland calls aid pledges of Western countries "stingy."

January 6
International aid conference convenes in Jakarta, Indonesia.

December 31: Death toll hits 150,000; United States increases aid pledge from $15 million to $350 million.

2005   **January 1:** Dr. David Nabarro, of the World Health Organization, warns that as many people could die of diseases as from the tsunami.

January 2: World Health Organization reports that diseases caused by contaminated drinking water are chief concerns.

January 3: Former U.S. presidents Bill Clinton and George H.W. Bush named to head international fund-raising effort.

January 19
Death toll exceeds 210,000.

May 20
Scientists revise earthquake's magnitude to 9.2, second most powerful ever recorded.

August
Indian Ocean tsunami warning system approved at UNESCO meeting.

2006

February 13
Health officials report that epidemics of disease seem to have been avoided.

December 1
First tsunami warning buoy launched in Indian Ocean.

January 5: U.S. Secretary of State Colin Powell views damage in Indonesia.

January 6: International aid conference convenes in Jakarta, Indonesia.

January 13: United Nations's Egeland says threat of epidemic diseases has been reduced.

January 19: Death toll exceeds 210,000.

February 13: Health officials report that epidemics of disease seem to have been avoided.

March 28: Earthquake of 8.7 magnitude occurs near December site; no tsunami results from it.

May 19: Earthquake of 6.9 magnitude occurs off Sumatran coast; no tsunami results.

May 20: Scientists revise earthquake's magnitude to 9.2, second most powerful ever recorded.

August: Indian Ocean tsunami warning system approved at UNESCO meeting.

December 26: Siren and moment of silence in Banda Aceh, Indonesia, mark tsunami's first anniversary.

2006   **June 28:** UNESCO says Indian Ocean tsunami warning system "up and running."

December 1: First tsunami warning buoy launched in Indian Ocean.

December 6: Oxfam says more than 25,000 families still homeless in Indonesia's Aceh province.

Glossary

apocalypse Any universal or widespread destruction or disaster.

axis The line about which a rotating body, such as the Earth, turns.

black market The buying and selling of goods in violation of laws or regulations.

buoy A distinctively shaped and marked float, sometimes carrying a signal or signals, anchored to mark a channel, anchorage, navigational hazard, etc.

communicable Transmittable between persons or species; contagious.

cricket A ball and bat game played chiefly in the United Kingdom and in former British colonies.

debris The remains of anything broken down or destroyed; ruins; rubble.

epicenter The central point of an event such as an earthquake.

fault zone The area around a break or series of breaks in a body of rock.

geophysicist One who studies the physical properties of the Earth and its atmosphere.

gross national product (GNP) The total economic value of a country's goods and services for one year.

minaret A tower or turret attached to a mosque from which people are called to prayer.

mosque A Muslim house of worship.

obstetrician Physicians who specialize in the delivery of babies.

sediment   Any material that settles to the bottom of a liquid; in geology, solid matter that is carried and deposited by water or ice.

seismograph   A device used for measuring the strength of an earthquake.

seismologist   One who studies earthquakes and the mechanical properties of the Earth.

tectonic   Forces causing movement of the Earth's crust.

tsunami   Powerful wave or series of waves resulting from a major disturbance of the ocean's surface.

Bibliography

Aglionby, John. "Stench of dead bodies is all around. There's no time to identify them—just take them to mass graves," *Guardian*, December 31, 2004. Available online. URL: http://www.guardian.co.uk/tsunami/story/0,15671,1381289,00.html. Downloaded on December 7, 2006.

Allen, Richard. "Next tsunami 'will hit within 50 years,'" *London Times*, January 18, 2005. Available online. URL: http://www.timesonline.co.uk/tol/news/world/article413932.ece. Downloaded on January 29, 2007.

"Bad water, disease threaten tsunami survivors," MSNBC News, January 3, 2005. Available online. URL: http://www.msnbc.msn.com/id/6755980. Downloaded on January 16, 2007.

Baker, Peter, and Alan Cooperman. "Bush puts father, Clinton to work," *Washington Post*, January 4, 2005. Available online. URL: http://www.washingtonpost.com/wp-dyn/articles/A44260-2005Jan3.html. Downloaded on February 3, 2007.

Benton, Pat. "Three Days of Hell in Khao Lak," Tsunami Survivor Stories, July 27, 2005. Available online. URL: http://www.tsunamistories.net/ViewStory.aspx?StoryID=142b076b-d682-48ce-944b-d2c5877ea471. Downloaded on November 28, 2006.

Bidawi, Praful. "Tsunami Impact: Loss of Innocence in the Politics of Aid," Common Dreams, January 5, 2005. Available online. URL: http://www.commondreams.org/headlines05/0105-10.htm. Downloaded on January 12, 2007.

Bowman, Naomi. "Survivor," Tsunami Survivor Stories, June 18, 2005. Available online. URL: http://phukettsunami.blogspot.com/2005/06/survivor-naomi-bowman.html. Downloaded on November 28, 2006.

"Build logistics, cooperation before next tsunami," Scoop News Service, January 31, 2005. Available online. URL: http://www

.scoop,co.nz/mason/stories/WO0501/S00343.htm. Downloaded on February 24, 2007.

Burke, Chris. "A Tsunami Survivor's Story," *Pacific*, Summer 2005. Available online. URL: http://www.pacificu.edu/magazine/2005/summer/tsunami-survivor.cfm. Downloaded on November 28, 2006.

Cascio, Jamais. "The Tsunami Next Time," World Changing, December 28, 2004. Available online. URL: http://www.worldchanging.com/archives/001828.html. Downloaded on January 29, 2007.

Chakravarti, Sunetra, and Stephen Farrell. "When the water receded, the cricketers were gone," *London Times*, December 28, 2004. Available online. URL: http://www.timesonline.co.uk/tol/news/world/article406336.ece. Downloaded on December 8, 2006.

Chesshyre, Tom. "After the horror, disaster zones will want tourists to return," *London Times*, January 1, 2005. Available online. URL: http://ezp.tccd.edu:2367/ehost/detail?vid=23&hid=13&sid=b2e2fc04-9fc7-4bea-ae7d-052a5310f36e%40sessionmgr7. Downloaded December 8, 2006.

"Colleen McGinn." Ohio University Honors Tutorial College. Available online. URL: http://www.honors.ohio.edu/ColleenM.htm. Downloaded on January 25, 2007.

Cox, Jean. "Surviving parents—and the story of a daughter who did not—Leanne Cox," Tsunami Survivor Stories, February 23, 2005. Available online. URL: http://phukettsunami.blogspot.com/2005/11/surviving-parents-and-story-of.html. Downloaded on November 28, 2006.

"Disease May Double Tsunami Toll," Fox News, December 29, 2004. Available online. URL: http://www.foxnews.com/story/o,2933,142759,00.html. Downloaded on January 16, 2007.

Drummond, Andrew. "Hope fades for lost children's parents as resorts are evacuated," *London Times*, December 28, 2004. Available online. URL: http://www.timesonline.co.uk/tol/

news/world/article406333.ece. Downloaded on December 8, 2006.

Drummond, Andrew. "Luxury resorts where bodies of tourists litter the beach," *London Times*, December 29, 2004. Available online. URL: http://www.timesonline.co.uk/tol/news/world/article406599.ece. Downloaded on December 8, 2006.

Elegant, Simon. "A City of Debris and Corpses," *TIME*, January 10, 2005. Available online. URL: http://www.time.com/time/magazine/article/0,9171,1013249,00.html. Downloaded on December 8, 2006.

Elliott, Michael. "Sea of Sorrow," *TIME*, January 2, 2005. Available online. URL: http://www.time.com/time/magazine/article/0,9171,1013255,00.html. Downloaded on December 8, 2006.

"Eyewitness: Loss and despair in Aceh," BBC News, January 4, 2005. Available online. URL: http://news.bbc.co.uk/2/hi/asia-pacific/4145859.stm. Downloaded on December 5, 2006.

"Experts Try to Predict What the Next Tsunami Will Do," Planet Ark World Environment News, October 2, 2005. Available online. URL: http://www.planetark.com/advantgo/dailynewsstory.cfm?newsid=29454. Downloaded on January 29, 2007.

"Ex-presidents launch private aid effort," Cable News Network, January 4, 2005. Available online. URL: http://www.cnn.com/2005/US/01/03/tsunami.presidents. Downloaded February 3, 2007.

"Felix, Louise & Zac in Phi Phi," Tsunami Survivor Stories, May 11, 2005. Available online. URL: http://phukettsunami.blogspot.com/2005/05/survivor-felix-louise-and-zac.html. Downloaded on November 28, 2006.

Hawkes, Nigel. "Dirty water now poses biggest risk to survivors," *London Times*, December 28, 2004. Available online. URL: http://www.timesonline.co.uk/tol/news/world/article406340.ece. Downloaded on December 8, 2007.

Hawkes, Nigel. "Early alarm could have saved thousands of lives," *London Times*, December 28, 2004. Available online. URL: http://www.timesonline.co.uk/tol/news/world/article406354.ece. Downloaded December 12, 2006.

Hankwerk, Brian. "Tsunami Redraws Indian Ocean Maps," *National Geographic*, January 12, 2005. Available online. URL: http://news.nationalgeographic.com/news/2005/01/0112_050112_tv_tsunami_map.html. Downloaded on November 28, 2006.

Hoogenkamp, Dennis. "Survivor," Tsunami Survivor Stories, November 15, 2005. Available online. URL: http://phukett-sunami.blogspot.com/2005/12/survivor-dennis-hoogenkamp.html. Downloaded on November 28, 2006.

Huyton, Saly. "Survivor," Tsunami Survivor Stories, August 14, 2005. Available online. URL: http://phukettsunami.blogspot.com/2005/08/survivor-saly-huyton.html. Downloaded on November 28, 2006.

"Indonesia: Aroma of success surrounds tsunami survivor's coffee shop," Relief Web, October 31, 2006. Available online. URL: http://www.reliefweb.int/rw/RWB.NSF/db900SID/KHII-6V48HJ?OpenDocument. Downloaded on November 28, 2006.

Jean, Grace. "Indian Ocean Tsunami Warning System to Become Operational in 2006," *National Defense*, November 2005. Available online. URL: http://www.nationaldefensemagazine.org/issues/2005/Nov/Indian_Ocean.htm. Downloaded on February 2, 2007.

de Jone, Kaz, Sue Prosser, and Nathan Ford. "Addressing Psychosocial Needs in the Aftermath of the Tsunami," PubMed Central, June 28, 2005. Available online. URL: http://www.pubmedcentral.nih.gov/articlerender.fcgi?artid=1160584. Downloaded on January 16, 2007.

Kessler, Franz L. "Where Will The Next Tsunami Hit?," Author's Den, December 31, 2004. Available online. URL: http://www.

authorsden.com/visit/viewarticle.asp?AuthorID=14304&id=16492. Downloaded on January 29, 2007.

Kimar, Kumar, and Sasi Kimar "Tsunami survivors in southern India speak to the WSWS," World Socialist Web site, January 21, 2005. Available online. URL: http://www.wsws.org/articles /2005/jan2005/indi-j21.shtml. Downloaded on December 5, 2006.

Lallanilla, Marc. "Doctors Debate Tsunami Health Impact," ABC News, January 6, 2005. Available online. URL: http:// abcnews.go.com/Health/Tsunami/story?id=387015&page=1. Downloaded on January 16, 2007.

Lang, Christine. "Tsunami Survivor Story," Travel and Transitions, 2005. Available online. URL: http://www.traveland transitions.com/your_stories/winners2006/honourable _mentions/tsunami_survivor_story.htm. Downloaded on November 28, 2006.

Lowe, Dave. "Survivor," Tsunami Survivor Stories, December 25, 2005. Available online. URL: http://phukettsunami. blogspot.com/2005/12/survivor-dave-lowe.html. Downloaded on November 28, 2006.

Loyd, Linda. "Drug companies donating supplies in unprecedented amounts," *Philadelphia Inquirer*, January 14, 2005. Quoted in *Tsunami: Hope, Heroes, and Incredible Stories of Survival*, Chicago: Triumph Books, 2005, p. 71.

Lype, George. "'I saw the sea eat my wife, kids,'" Rediff News Service, December 27, 2004. Available online. URL: http:// specials.rediff.com/news/2004/dec/27tsunami1.htm. Downloaded on December 7, 2006.

Macan-Markar, Marwaan. "Lack of Water-Borne Disease a Silent Success," Interpress Service News Agency, June 27, 2005. Available online. URL: http://ipsnews.net/interna. asp?idnews=29234. Downloaded on January 16, 2007.

MacKenzie, Deborah. "Dead bodies pose no epidemic threat, say experts," *NewScientist*, January 5, 2005. Available online.

URL: http://www.newscientist.com/article.ns?id=dn6849. Downloaded on January 16, 2007.

Maley, Jacqueline. "Second wave of horror in diseases," *Sydney Morning Herald*, January 1, 2005. Available online. URL: http://www.smh.com.au/news/Asia-Tsunami/Second-wave-of-horror-in-diseases/2004/12/31/1104344987704.html. Downloaded on January 16, 2007.

Marshall, Gary. "Survivor: Charley Marshall—Age 8," Tsunami Survivor Stories, June 21, 2005. Available online. URL: http://phukettsunami.blogspot.com/2005/06/survivor-charley-marshall-age-8.html. Downloaded on November 28, 2006.

McCall, William. "OSU researchers seek ways to withstand tsunamis," O.H. Hinsdale Wave Research Laboratory, Oregon State University, December 26, 2005. Available online. URL: http://wave.oregonstate.edu/news/story/1658. Downloaded on January 29, 2007.

McGrory, Daniel. "Scramble to name victims before they are buried," *London Times*, January 1, 2005. Available online. URL: http://www.timesonline.co.uk/tol/news/world/article407398.ece. Downloaded on December 8, 2006.

"Medium saw wave," *Sun*, January 3, 2006. Available online. URL: http://www.thesun.co.uk/article/0,2-2004600994,00.html. Downloaded on December 5, 2006.

"'A miracle' amid scramble for survivors," MSNBC News Services, December 28, 2004. Available online. URL: http://www.msnbc.msn.com/id6756725. Downloaded on November 28, 2006.

Morton, Cole. "Tsunami aftermath: Just ordinary people, on an ordinary day ... then," *Independent on Sunday*, January 2, 2005. Available online. URL: http://findarticles.com/p/articles/mi_qn4159/is_20050102/ai_n9698097. Downloaded on December 7, 2006.

Mott, Maryann. "Did Animals Sense Tsunami Was Coming?" *National Geographic*, January 4, 2005. Available online. URL:

http://news.nationalgeographic.com/news/2005/01/0104_ 050104_tsunami_animals.html. Downloaded on December 7, 2006.

Moulane, Hazil. "My father's body has been found, my mother is lost," *London Times*, January 1, 2005. Available online. URL: http://www.timesonline.co.uk/tol/news/world/article407399. ece. Downloaded on December 8, 2006.

"MSF: WHO Tsunami Disease Warning Sensationalized," Indonesia Relief, June 11, 2005. Available online. URL: http://www.indonesia-relief-org/mod.php?mod=bank&op=readnews=bankid=4&artid=1128. Downloaded on January 16, 2007.

Nakashima, Ellen. "Experts Fear Burma Was Battered," *Washington Post*, January 3, 2005. Available online. URL: http://www.washingtonpost.com/wp-dyn/articles/A43018-2005Jan2. html. Downloaded on December 8, 2006.

Naughton, Phillipe. "Asian tsunami death toll rises above 23,000, *Times*, December 27, 2004. Available online. URL: http://www.tsunamistories.net/ViewStory.aspx?StoryID=142b076b-d682-48ce-944b-d2c5877ea471. Downloaded on December 5, 2006.

Neff, Nancy. "Waves of Relief," University of Texas at Austin, July 11, 2005. Available online. URL: http://www.utexas.edu/features/2005/tsunami/index.html. Downloaded on November 11, 2006.

"NOAA Emphasizes Need for Global Tsunami Warning System," NOAA News Online, March 30, 2005. Available online. URL: http://www.noaanews.noaa.gov/stories2005/s2411.htm. Downloaded on February 1, 2007.

Norton, Jerry. "Disease still a threat in tsunami-stricken Aceh—U.N.," Yahoo! India News, January 14, 2005. Available online. URL: http://in.news.yahoo.com/o50114/137/2j0ia. html. Downloaded on January 16, 2007.

"On Day Five of Tsunami Disaster, Extent of Death and Destruction Continues to Grow," transcript of Cable News Network's

American Morning, December 30, 2004. Available online. URL: http://transcripts.cnn.com/TRANSCRIPTS/0412/30/ ltm.06.html. Downloaded on December 6, 2005.

"Out of the blue, a deadly wall of water," *Guardian,* December 27, 2005. Available online. URL: http://www.guardian.co.uk/ naturaldisasters/story/0,7369,1380024,00.html. Downloaded on December 7, 2006.

Owen, James. "Tsunami Family Saved by Schoolgirl's Geography Lesson," *National Geographic,* January 18, 2005. Available online. URL: http://news.nationalgeographic.com/ news/2005/01/0118_050118_tsunami_geography_lesson. html. Downloaded on November 28, 2006.

Pagella, Sasha. "Penang," Tsunami Stories. Available online. URL: http://www.tsunamistories.net/ViewStory.aspx?StoryID =fc9988fc-1d07-4f96-bad0-ddb80dc49b29. Downloaded on November 28, 2006.

Parry, Richard Lloyd. "Where time is life, vital aid stands delayed at an airport," *London Times,* January 1, 2005. Available online. URL: http://www.timesonline.co.uk/tol/news/ world/article407396.ece. Downloaded on December 8, 2006.

Pellerin, Cheryl. "U.S. to Install Indian Ocean Tsunami-Detection Buoy in December," United States Department of State, August 21, 2006. Available online. URL: http://usinfo.state. gov/xarchives/display.html?p=washfile-english&y=2006& m=August&x=20060821074802lcnirellep0.7738916. Downloaded on January 29, 2007.

———. "U.S., Thai Officials Celebrate Tsunami-Detection Device Launch," United States Department of State, December 1, 2006. Available online. URL: http://usinfo.state.gov/ xarchives/display.html?p=washfile-english&y=2006&m= December&x=20061201110037cmretrop0.6052667. Downloaded on January 29, 2007.

Pepper, Barrie. "Changing the Beer Into Water." Tsunami Stories, January 19, 2005. Available online. URL: http://www.

tsunamistories.net/ViewStory.aspx?StoryID=fcf4913f-7dcf-4054-bca0-65332105231c. Downloaded on November 28, 2006.

Philip, Catherine. "No one is left in the fishing village swallowed up by the sea," *London Times*, January 1, 2005. Available online. URL: http://www.timesonline.co.uk/tol/news/world/article407448.ece. Downloaded on December 8, 2006.

———. "They lost everything. Now they are losing even the will to live," *London Times*, January 5, 2005. Available online. URL: http://www.timesonline.co.uk/tol/news/world/article408483.ece. Downloaded on December 8, 2006.

Powell, Bill. "After the Flood," *TIME*, January 10, 2005. Available online. URL: http://www.time.com/time/magazine/article/0,9171,1013261,00.html. Downloaded on December 8, 2006.

Rama, Lakshmi. "My Boat Is Nothing But Scrap," *Washington Post*, January 16, 2005. Available online. URL: http://www.washingtonpost.com/wp-dyn/articles/A12532-2005Jan15.html. Downloaded on December 8, 2006.

Redwood, Lynda J., and Louis Riddez. "Post-Tsunami Medical Care: Health Problems Encountered in the International Committee of the Red Cross Hospital in Banda Aceh, Indonesia," University of Wisconsin, *Prehospital and Disaster Medicine* 21, no. 1 (January–February 2006). Available online. URL: http://pdm.medicine.wisc.edu/21-1%20PDFs/redwood.pdf. Downloaded on January 16, 2007.

Revkin, Andrew. "Tragedy in real time," *Age*, January 28, 2005. Available online. URL: http://www.theage.com.au/articles/2005/01/07/1104832307389.html?oneclick=true. Downloaded on December 6, 2006.

Richardson, Bennett. "New push for tsunami-alert system," *Christian Science Monitor*, December 29, 2004. Available online. URL: http://www.csmonitor.com/2004/1229/p01s03-woap.htm. Downloaded on January 30, 2007.

Ryan, Caroline. "How tsunami diseases were curbed," BBC News, March 22, 2005. Available online. URL: http://news.

bbc.co.uk/2/hi/health/4355897.stm. Downloaded on January 16, 2007.

"SA tsunami survivor recounts terror," Mail and Guardian Online, December 31, 2004. Available online. URL: http://www.mg.co.za/articlepage.aspx?area=/breaking_news/breaking_news__national&articleid=194390. Downloaded on November 28, 2006.

Sample, Ian. "Hollywood fantasy? Tidal wave disaster is just waiting to happen," *Guardian*, August 10, 2004. Available online. URL: http://www.guardian.co.uk/uk_news/story/0,3604,1279710,00.html. Downloaded on December 6, 2006.

Samuels, Lennox. "Marines arrive in Sri Lanka to deliver tsunami aid," *Dallas Morning News*, January 6, 2005. Quoted in *Tsunami: Hope, Heroes, and Incredible Stories of Survival*, Chicago: Triumph Books, 2005, p. 42.

"Scientists say next tsunami simply a matter of time," Newsfox Press Distribution, June 17, 2005. Available online. URL: http://www.newsfox.com/pte.mc?pte=050617020. Downloaded on January 29, 2007.

"Search for the perfect wave ended in disaster," *Independent*, January 1, 2005. Available online. URL: http://www.int.iol.co.za/index.php?set_id=1&click_id=3&art_id=vn20050101104609162C683332. Downloaded on December 7, 2006.

Shafeeq, Mohammed. "India reels in anguish," *Newsday*, December 28, 2004. Available online. URL: http://www.newsday.com/news/nationworld/ny-woindi284097972dec28,0,263386.story. Downloaded on December 5, 2006.

Simmonds, Luke. "First Hand Story," Tsunami Survivor Stories, December 30, 2004. Available online. URL: http://phukettsunami.blogspot.com/2004/12/first-hand-story-luke-simmonds.html. Downloaded on November 28, 2006.

Sipress, Alan. "Signs of Renewal Emerge in Indonesia," *Washington Post*, January 3, 2005. Available online. URL: http://www.

washingtonpost.com/wp-dyn/articles/A42963-2005Jan2.
html. Downloaded on December 8, 2006.

Stephens, Tim. "Seismologists publish detailed analysis of the great Sumatra-Andaman earthquake," *Currents*, May 23, 2005. Available online. URL: http://currents.ucsc.edu/04-05/05-23/science.asp. Downloaded on November 28, 2006.

Stott, Phillip. "It is man-made failings that allow natural disasters to wreak havoc," *London Times*, December 29, 2004. Available online. URL: http://www.timesonline.co.uk/tol/comment/columnists/guest_contributors/article406569.ece. Downloaded on December 8, 2006.

Thomas, Evan, and George Wehrfritz. "Tide of Grief," *Newsweek*, January 4, 2005. Available online. URL: http://www.msnbc.msn.com/id/6777595/site/newsweek. Downloaded on November 28, 2006.

"Traumatized tsunami survivor takes his life," *Independent*, May 21, 2005. Available online. URL: http://www.int.iol.co.za/index.php?set_id=1&click_id=2985&art_id=qwl116656288752R131. Downloaded on November 28, 2006.

"Tsunami alert," transcript of Public Broadcasting System program *NewsHour*, January 11, 2005. Available online. URL: http://www.pbs.org/newshour/bb/science/jan-june05/tsunami_1-11.html. Downloaded on December 6, 2006.

Tsunami: Hope, Heroes and Incredible Stories of Survival. Chicago: Triumph Books, 2005.

"Tsunami memories linger," *Bangkok Post*, December 24, 2006. Available online. URL: http://www.bangkokpost.com/tsunami.php?id=115427. Downloaded on January 29, 2007.

"Tsunami: Readers' eyewitness accounts," BBC News, January 6, 2005. Available online. URL: http://news.bbc.co.uk/2/hi/talking_point/4146031.stm. Downloaded on December 4, 2006.

"Tsunami's 'second wave of death'—disease—can now be largely avoided, UN says," UN News Centre, January 16, 2007. Available online. URL: http://www.un.org/apps/news/story.

asp?NewsID=13037&Cr=tsunami&Crl=. Downloaded on January 16, 2007.

"Tsunami Survivor's 15 Days at Sea," CBS News, January 11, 2005. Available online. URL: http://www.cbsnews.com/stories/2005/01/11/world/main666238.shtml. Downloaded on November 28, 2006.

"Tsunami survivors face disease, starvation," *Sydney Morning Herald*, December 29, 2004. Available online. URL: http://www.smh.com.au/news/Asia-Tsunami/Tsunami-survivors-face-disease-starvation/2004/12/28/1103996558253.html. Downloaded on January 16, 2007.

"Tsunami wreaks mental havoc," World Health Organization, June 1, 2005. Available online. URL: http://www.who.int/bulletin/volumes/83/6/infocus0605/en/index.html. Downloaded on November 11, 2006.

"Tsunami Zone Spared Major Disease Outbreaks," Environment News Service, February 11, 2005. Available online. URL: http://www.ens-newswire.com/ens/feb2005/2005-02-11-01.asp. Downloaded on January 16, 2007.

Tucker, Neely. "In Sri Lanka, a New Wave of Pain," *Washington Post*, January 7, 2005. Available online. URL: http://www.washingtonpost.com/wp-dyn/articles/A54603-2005Jan6.html. Downloaded on December 8, 2006.

Tyson, Peter. "Wave of the Future," Public Broadcasting System, Wave That Shook the World, March 2005. Available online. URL: http://www.pbs.org/wgbh/nova/tsunami/wave/html. Downloaded on January 29, 2007.

"Vow to restore Tamil Nadu fleet," BBC News, January 5, 2005. Available online. URL: http://news.bbc.co.uk/2/hi/south_asia/4149471.stm. Downloaded on December 7, 2006.

"Wave that shook the world," transcript of Public Broadcasting System program *NOVA*, March 29, 2005. Available online. URL: http://www.pbs.org/wgbh/nova/transcripts/3208_tsunami.html. Downloaded on December 6, 2006.

"When will next tsunami strike?" MSNBC News, June 29, 2005. Available online. URL: http://www.msnbc.msn.com/id/8379571. Downloaded on January 29, 2007.

"The world digs deep," *London Times*, December 31, 2004. Available online. URL: http://www.timesonline.co.uk/tol/news/world/article407117.ece. Downloaded on December 8, 2006.

Further Reading

BOOKS

Bindra, Satinder. *Tsunami: 7 Hours That Shook the World.* New Denli, India: HarperCollins Publishers India, 2005. This cooperative venture between HarperCollins India and the India Today newspaper group looks at the 2004 tsunami from the Indian point of view.

Blackhall, Susan. *Tsunami.* Cobham, UK: TAJ Books, 2005. Explores the history and causes of tsunamis and relates the extent of damage done by the 2004 Indian Ocean tsunami and subsequent aid efforts.

Reed, Jennifer. *Earthquakes: Disater & Survival.* Aldershot, UK: Enslow Publishers, 2005. Recounts some of history's most powerful earthquakes, including the one that caused the 2004 tsunami.

Rooney, Anne. *Tsunami.* North Mankato, Minn.: Arcturus Publications, 2007. Comprehensive account of the Indian Ocean tsunami for younger readers.

Stewart, Gail. *Catastrophe in Southern Asia: The Tsunami of 2004.* Detroit: Lucent Books, 2005. Excellent overall account of the tsunami from its causes to the worldwide effort to provide aid to the survivors.

Tibballs, Geoff. *Tsunami: The Most Terrifying Natural Disaster.* London: Carlton Books, 2005. Country-by-country account of the tsunami's destruction. All funds from the sale of this book went toward tsunami aid.

WEB SITES

Robin Good: Full Tsunami Video Footage, Pictures, Clips, and TV News Stories,
URL: http://www.masternewmedia.org/2005/01/02/full_tsunami_video_footage_pictures.htm.

Site makes it possible to go beyond reading about the
    tsunami and to actually see what it looked like.

Tsunami Survivor Stories,
URL: http://phukettsunami.blogspot.com.
First-person stories of those who survived the Indian Ocean
    tsunami make compelling reading.

Tsunamis.com,
URL: http://www.tsunamis.com.
This Project Care site provides a wide extent of information on
    the 2004 tsunami, including a selection of photographs.

Tsunami!
URL: http://www.ess.washington.edu/tsunami/index.html.
This site, hosted and maintained at the University of
    Washington by the Department of Earth and Space
    Sciences, does an excellent job of explaining what a
    tsunami is and also provides links to several other sites.

Picture Credits

Index

About the Author

WILLIAM W. LACE is a native of Fort Worth, Texas, where he is executive assistant to the chancellor at Tarrant County College. He holds a bachelor's degree from Texas Christian University, a master's degree from East Texas State University, and a doctorate from the University of North Texas. Prior to joining Tarrant County College, he was director of the News Service at the University of Texas at Arlington and a sportswriter and columnist for the *Fort Worth Star-Telegram*. He has written more than 40 nonfiction books for young readers on subjects ranging from the atomic bomb to the Dallas Cowboys. He and his wife, Laura, a retired school librarian, live in Arlington, Texas, and have two children and four grandchildren.